The
GOD
Who Intervenes

Embracing the Present Day Work
of the Holy Spirit in Your Life

KEITH TUCCI

FIRST EDITION

ISBN: 978-1-946466-61-7

Library of Congress Control Number: 2021907387

Published by

3741 Linden Avenue SE | Grand Rapids, MI 49548

Printed in the United States

Endorsements

Keith Tucci has not only been transformed by Jesus, he has allowed God to use him to bring that same transformation to others around the world. His willingness to be used by God in any kind of situation is inspiring and has impacted people, churches, cities, and even nations. Keith has lived a life surrendered to God. The wisdom that comes with that kind of a life is priceless.

—Pastor Eric Johns
Buffalo Dream Center, Buffalo, New York

Although I've known of Keith Tucci for over 35 years, I have only had the honor and privilege of a deeper friendship with him in the past few years. When I read *The God Who Intervenes,* I found myself choking up. I had no idea this incredible pastor, husband, father, and leader started life is such despair. Naturally speaking, Keith was destined to become another statistic and die a violent death at a young age. God obviously had other plans. The story of how God found and rescued Keith, gave him Penny and an amazing family, makes me love and worship Him more deeply. This book will help you lean into a God that loves you, beyond your circumstances, pain, and limits. You will be compelled to expect that the same God who liberated and grew Keith into a "Father in the Faith," can take you to your God-ordained finish line.

—Pastor John Nuzzo
Victory Family Church, Cranberry Township, Pennsylvania

Keith Tucci is a trophy of God's transforming power! God raised him up from painful beginnings to be a prophetic voice to his generation. Keith is a treasure to Christ's Church!

—Pastor Ron Johnson Jr.
Living Stones Church, Crown Point, Indiana

Keith Tucci has helped more pastors and churches overcome the trials and fires of life than any man I've ever known. As a personal friend and mentor for over 30 years, I value what he says and how he leads. *The God Who Intervenes* is loaded with insights that will help any Christian be alert for God's interventions, and walk successfully in Christ.

—Pastor Joe Warner
Prophetic Voice Churches & Ministries, Yadkinville, North Carolina

I have known Keith Tucci for almost 30 years. During our times together it is very apparent the passion Keith has for our Lord Jesus Christ. The passion could only be rooted in a deeply personal encounter with Jesus.

As a young boy on the streets of Pittsburgh, he encountered a group of older women who began to pray for him. Their prayers brought into existence the great purposes God had decreed over his life. I believe the life of Keith Tucci is a living epistle demonstrating the power of prayer and the power of God's grace. Keith's life paints a beautiful picture of how high, how wide, and how deep God's love is for us.

—Pastor Brian Lother
Hope Community Church, Corcoran, Minnesota

It is absolutely amazing how God took a fatherless boy, shunned by family, friends, and teachers, and molded him into a man of impeccable character, grace, and grit, to make Himself known to the whole world. Keith's life is a "living parable" of what God can do in a life totally devoted to Him.

He candidly, honestly, and humorously reveals instances in his life where the providential hand of God was clearly at work in him. Guiding him. Encouraging him. Keeping his head when others were losing theirs.

The history of God's dealings with Keith is fascinating. First to bring him to Himself, then set him up as a pastor, later to introduce him to our nation as a leader in Operation Rescue and ultimately its director. Not done, God introduced him to the jail population in America and then promoted him to international ministries around the world. The theology of heaven bursts forth and becomes biography on earth. This is the way the "God Who Intervenes" has chosen to touch the lives of men.

—Pastor Flip Benham
Former Director of Operation Rescue America

I have been in a thirty-three year covenant relationship with Keith Tucci. His life and heart are full of revelation knowledge and wisdom. He is the voice of one crying out for Repentance, Redemption, and Restoration. Read his heartfelt thoughts in this book and be encouraged.

—Pastor Rod Aguillard
Network of Related Pastors, Reserve, Louisiana

What a man preaches and writes flows from his very being. For over 20 years, I've been challenged and strengthened every time I've heard Keith Tucci minister. This book will be instrumental in helping people see that God is involved in their lives for the better, even when they don't see it.

—Pastor Troy Thomas
Bethel Church, Vidalia, Louisiana

I was intrigued to read *The God Who Intervenes*, written by my long time dear friend and companion in the cause of Christ, Keith Tucci. From our early days of ministering, preaching and serving in the former Soviet Union, to standing side by side in defense of life, God's intervention has unlocked and opened doors no man alone or system of government could keep closed. The verse that comes to mind is: "Are not two sparrows sold for a copper coin? And not one of them falls to the ground apart from your Father's will. But the very hairs on your head are all numbered. Do not fear therefore; you are of more value than many sparrows" (Matthew 10:29-31).

—Pastor Joe Kelly

Hamptons Church, Sag Harbor, New York

Table of Contents

Foreword

The stories in *The God Who Intervenes* are going to open up your eyes to see how God can and will intervene in your life when you are simply living out your faith daily. God has done remarkable things with and through Keith Tucci over the past decades, and his life story is sure to help you see the supernatural be a part of your daily life!

Keith is one of the most influential men in my life. He has helped fashion and form me into the pastor and leader I am today. He consistently challenges the people and leaders of Jesus' church to live up to their fullest potential as salt and light in their communities, country, and world. His life is a demonstration of faith and fullness of what God can do through someone who is totally dependent upon Him.

I met Keith when I was 18 years old, and ever since the first day we spoke, he has lit a fire in my heart to serve and see Jesus be the head of His church. He has been one of the most confrontational, inspirational, intimidating, and prophetic men I have ever met!

I remember the day he first pulled up in front of my house and asked me to go for a ride. As we drove around the east suburbs of Pittsburgh, he shared with me a vision and picture of what Jesus' church could look like. I still remember my heart pounding and my hands sweaty with fear, excitement, and joy all at the same time, thinking I could be a part of this move of God! It was one week later that I began serving in my church, which only had about not twenty people. And here I am now as the pastor of that same church, nearly four decades later. This is the only church I have ever been a part of, mainly due to the foundation and ministry of Keith.

I have a strong bias for action over discussion and clear direction over discourse. I learned that from Keith's ministry. I remember listening to his contagious conviction over the abortion issue, which led me, along with hundreds of others, to be arrested several times in different states, all because something needed to be done about this abomination in our country. There is always a method to his movement—he clearly sees problems as opportunities. We will never know how many people are alive today, all because of Keith's ministry.

Keith made a decision to go to the Soviet Union when it wasn't safe, cool, or timely in the life of our church. But when God spoke, he obeyed. He was available and determined to be faithful to whatever and wherever God called him. This allowed people in our church an opportunity to step up, and fulfill God's call in their own lives.

An experience that forever affected my life, was when I saw our church of 75 people raise over $75,000 cash in one offering for a new building. Keith envisioned us. To this day, this is still something that has forever marked me. This building that we bought was an old, dilapidated school building that was in such bad shape that even kids stopped breaking into it because there was nothing left to destroy, burn, or break. And yet, this is the building that we have launched several churches and campuses out of to this day. This all happened because God intervened!

Watching Keith and his wife, Penny, serve and sacrifice together, has been a real blessing. Together, they have gone against the grain of society in the size of their family (eight children) and served God through difficult circumstances. They have moved, lived in different states, and together have made a big difference for God's purposes. I have seen firsthand that every time God intervened, Penny was by Keith's side, hearing, believing, and stepping out with him!

Three things I have learned from Keith's lifestyle:

First, is what it really means to be Holy-Spirit led. When Keith hears God about going to a foreign country, starting a local project, or starting a new initiative, he acts. He is in love with "what-has-God-said?" and knows that the "how" will come later. *The God Who Intervenes* is about how God leads us to do more than we could ever accomplish on our own.

Second, Keith also taught me about believing the best concerning people with whom he is serving. He is able to take those who serve around him, and see them accomplish far more than they ever thought possible, simply by demonstrating that he believed in them. Keith's mantra for others is, "Availability is your greatest ability." If you get around him, you are going to get in over your head, because after all, that is when God shows up. In *The God Who Intervenes* you will learn that God believes much more in us, than we even believe in ourselves.

Third, Keith has shown me what faithfulness to the call of God really looks like! If we'll simply do what God asks us to do, full of faith, God makes up difference. Without faith, it is impossible to please God. In *The God Who Intervenes* you will learn about the currency of faith and faithfulness.

As you read this book, get ready to see your faith go a whole new level as you experience God showing up in your daily life. The Holy Spirit is going to have you take some bold steps of faith, so I encourage you to not merely acknowledge Keith's story, but get ready for your own journey to take some twists and turns you might not have expected. God is like that! Make room for God to show up and the Holy Spirit to set you up. Jesus will help you step out to your supernatural lifestyle!

I am a better leader because of Keith's leadership, a better man because of his faithful example, and deeper follower of Christ because of the way he follows. And all of this because of God's story being written through Keith's life, and *The God Who Intervenes*.

— Pastor Rick Paladin
Bridge City Church, Pittsburgh, Pennsylvania

Why Spaghetti Is So Important

We had just gotten back to our rooms after church on Sunday. Our rooms at the Bible school were similar to those of an old roadside motel—which it once served as—with the typical two beds, a bath, and built-in drawers. What it didn't have was a kitchen, and the school had no eating facilities for the male students. The ladies were housed in the wing of the church that hosted our school. They had a kitchen in their wing, but no men were allowed in. How we were supposed to eat was left up to us.

There were a few restaurants around if you had a car and, of course, money. My car was covered with plastic in the parking lot. Actually it was a very nice vehicle. I was always a car guy. It was a 1970 Torino with a 429 engine and a four-speed transmission with a sharp paint job and a nice set of wheels and tires. I parked it behind the dorm, wiped it down with grease, and covered it with plastic. It was painful to watch it sit there while I hitchhiked, but there was no way to go to school and afford the car at the same time. I could not afford the insurance or the gas to drive it. After class each day I would hitchhike back and forth to the local K-Mart auto center, where I put on tires, mufflers, and shock absorbers; changed oil; and installed new batteries. This usually paid enough to at least buy a couple of meals a week and pay for school. We lived on peanut butter. Ironically, we were not allowed to have any cooking devices in our room. My roommate, Jim, and I were both hungry and broke. The school, as far as I know, just randomly stuck roommates together. Jim and I were probably the two poorest in the bunch. We were not much help to one another.

One Sunday after church, when we were particularly hungry and just plain tired of peanut butter, I knelt down beside the bed, grabbed Jim's hand, and said, "We're going to pray for a spaghetti dinner." As God is my judge, within seconds (before Jim's knees could even hit the floor) there was a knock on the door. When we opened it, we saw a couple we didn't know standing there. Their daughter, Sherry, was a student at our school. They lived several hours away and had decided to surprise her with a home-cooked spaghetti dinner! They had made enough for her roommates, but on this Sunday afternoon no one else was around! "Would you like some?" they asked. Jim looked at me in disbelief. I had to convince him that it was not a set-up. They opened the tail gate of their station wagon and slid out the thermoses of hot spaghetti and meatballs. There was also salad, bread, and homemade apple pie.

This really happened! After days of peanut butter, we were giddy. Jim asked them if I had known anything about it, but they didn't even know me! When I think back on that incident, I'm reminded of God's humor and His willingness to take care of me—and He always has! I tend to be a serious person. I've had to learn to take God and His work seriously, but not myself. Being able to laugh at yourself is one of the best signs that God's grace is actively working in you.

Maybe that's why even today, when Penny makes one of her Italian feasts and all the kids and grandkids come over, it's a very happy time in my life. I get a big smile on my face as I enjoy my spaghetti and meatballs.

How I ended up at the Bible school is much more miraculous than the Italian feast God sent Jim and me that day. I was raised—if you want to use that term—in various projects (Hawkins Village, Prospect Terrace, Dravosburg, and McKeesport) of Allegheny County (Pittsburgh), Pennsylvania. We would land in the projects after one of mom's failed marriages (which usually lasted only a few years). My mom was a very attractive lady but, as I would come to understand, a very broken woman. She married her first husband to get out of the house, away from an unkind mother.

My memories of my grandmother are of a self-centered person who resented us. I had to live with her for a while after my mom was in the hospital due to a beating she took from Cal, one of her soon-to-be-ex-husbands. That experience was marked by the night she put me, my older brother, Lee, and my sister, Debbie, in a cab and sent us to our birth father's house unannounced! We had not seen him in several years. I was eight years old. What happened next was unpleasant—Lee got slapped across the face. He would have been about thirteen years old at the time and was as quiet and passive as I was wild and rebellious. Our family issues had affected us, resulting in totally different outcomes. It's important when we are ministering to folks that we go beyond psychological profiles and assessments and depend on the Holy Spirit. We were raised in the same environment with totally different effects. We would both come to salvation ten years later, miles apart, not really in contact with each other and through two different groups of people.

That day apparently Grandma had told Lee what to say to our dad. This included a demand for the cab to be paid for. My heart still feels the pain of the shy, shrinking boy being belted across the face by our dad. The cab driver witnessed this while waiting for his payment. He then jumped back into his cab and raced back to Grandma's house to report what he had seen and no doubt also to get paid. He then returned to get us. All the while, we stood in the living room terrified and unwanted by our father and our grandmother. As noted, our mom was in the hospital.

My sister, who would have been the most consistent person in my life, came to salvation about a year after Lee and I did. She is truly an amazing person. She and her husband, Steve, always showed kindness and support to me. Steve's mom and dad were also kind to me and invited me to their own family events as I tagged along with them even before they were married. Actually it's pretty remarkable when you think about it—that a young couple would include their troubled younger brother. Debbie was the one who would check on me in my wildest and craziest days and showed consistent care and concern. I'll be forever grateful for her love and support.

At one point I tried to join the army. In those days if you had a pulse you could get in. I guess she knew that would have been a disaster for me. She intercepted the mail and phone calls to prevent me from going. I didn't find out until much later. I had a blood condition that affected my complexion. She paid for me to go to a dermatologist. The fact that she was pretty and well liked also helped me with the older guys who wanted to be my friend in hopes of getting close to her. The effects of how we live no doubt, distorted everything about family and love. Can you imagine how difficult that would be?—I think even more so for a little girl. Debbie is another example of the grace of God: being a great wife, a committed mother to her three children, and later her grandchildren.

2

Fighting for Your Life

Part of the reason that the spaghetti dinner sticks out in my mind and even brings me comfort still today is that it seems eating was always a challenge. At a young age I became a regular shoplifter. Food was my primary target. It wasn't until a few years later that my mom started drinking. Things went from bad to worse. I got a "job" through one of the county agencies that tried to help poor families. I was in ninth grade. I would walk from my school to the grade school, where my job was to help the janitor for two and a half hours each day. One of my responsibilities was to empty the garbage in a group of classrooms. These were the days when young students ate at their desks. I discovered a gold mine—bags of food tossed away. Each day I would sift through the cans and find perfectly good sandwiches that had not been touched.

As if there weren't enough junk in my life, I started drinking and doing street drugs. This only amped up my aggression. I was already a fighter, having been in nine schools by seventh grade; you learn that the new kid has to talk with his fist, not just his wits. I definitely got beat up more than once, but my goal was for them to never come back for more. It seemed to work.

When our school (East Pittsburgh High School) merged with Turtle

Creek High School, an incident happened that pretty much caused people to stay out of my way after that. Mark was an overweight kid who also came from a very poor background. He and his mom (who had him late in life) lived in a converted attic of an apartment building that had no bathroom. They had to go to the hallway downstairs, where they shared a bathroom with the people below them. Mark and his mom were alone; they had no other family. After the merger the resident alpha male, Dave, proceeded to pick on and humiliate Mark. One day I had had enough. I told him in front of others to stop. He asked, "Who's going to make me?" Before I knew it, I told him I was that person! He said he would see me at lunchtime.

I had been in enough fights to know that I was in trouble. I still remember going into the bathroom and being sick. Getting beat up would be bad enough, but adding in the new school merger and all the tension with that would be utterly humiliating. When I walked out of the school at lunchtime, I did not have to guess where he was. It seemed as if the whole student body were waiting. They had formed a large circle at the edge of the school campus. Dave (whose nickname was "Hitch") was in the middle.

He was a muscle-bound guy who was feared by all. I was taller than he was, and after he came at me, I quickly realized my arms were longer than his. I was able to land a couple of hard shots, which stunned him. I'm sure that he thought that this skinny kid from East Pittsburgh was easy picking. My strategy was to keep him from getting his hands around me, because I knew he would squeeze me like a tube of toothpaste. As keen as I was not to let that happen, he was determined to get to me, which led him to make a desperate dive. This resulted in a flurry of my fists—I could tell the crowd was shocked. There was silence. The few who rooted for me had done so almost apologetically. When I drew blood I believe he got desperate. Though he was much stronger than me, it was obvious to me that I had more fights under my belt. Once my initial fear left, a rage began pouring out of me. Now I was really going after him. At the end he had fallen to his knees, his face and my hands and arms covered in blood. Finally his friends stepped in and carried him off to get medical attention.

The rage I had exhibited left the students stunned. Only a few of them spoke to me after the fight. Dave was not well liked by the administration, while I was an unknown entity at that time. Several teachers made a comment to me about the tree that Dave had run into. That was the story they told to the school nurse. Ironically, while we never became great friends, he would tell others about the whipping he took. Some years later after I had become a Christian, I ran into him. He introduced me to the girl he was with as that guy who beat him up. Now I was embarrassed about it—since I was a different person. I would continue struggling with anger as a personal sin, but that intense rage was no longer there.

It's interesting looking back. I had gotten into that situation by sticking up for the fat kid, whom people would punch in the arm to see how big of a bruise they could put on him. In some ways I was probably fighting for myself, identifying with the hurting and the lonely. Even as a heathen I had a pattern of defending the weak against the bullies. The devil is a counterfeiter who cannot create gifts or callings. He just tries to hijack them, as I've seen him attempt with my own children. I do think you have to punch the devil in the face like a bully; he seeks the path of least resistance. God is the giver of gifts and we are designed for His glory. Take a look at the music industry; some of the most popular and charismatic singers and bands come from Christian families. The devil hijacked their anointing as he directed them into pop culture. I think in the music arena it's very prominent, because Lucifer was once a "worship leader" (angel) himself.

At the time of the fight with Dave I had basically left home and lived here and there—nowhere really. I found an apartment building with a back room in the basement and spent a lot of my time there. I helped a tow truck driver by doing odds and ends for him. He had some damaged cars and I swung a deal to get a '68 Mercury Monterey. It was rough around the edges but proved to be a good vehicle to drive—but also to stay in.

The ladies who led me to Christ would find me in the car where I had parked overnight and would bring me breakfast. Actually they also invited me into their homes. My mom and I had become mostly estranged. She was broken; I was wild.

Several years earlier I had gotten into a confrontation with my youngest brother, Dale. Like my oldest brother, Chris, we had different dads, but, unlike Chris, we had been raised together. Chris had been involved as a getaway driver in an armed robbery, and in those days the judges gave you a choice—the army or jail. Chris joined the army and did very well, serving twelve years with distinction. I was only about eight at the time. We were back in the projects; this was after my mom had gotten out of the hospital. I remember the day he left, and we would never be close for a long time after that due to the fact that he lived in various places of the world and had his own family to care for. After Chris went away, Lee, Debbie, and I were left with no dad, no interested uncles, no other family or friends—basically no one who took an interest in us.

Dale was just a baby at the time, but his dad did stay involved in his life, supported him, and spent time with him. His dad, Cal, is the only guy who ever took any real time with me—helping me to learn athletics and including me in some of his times with Dale. Later in life I had an opportunity to come alongside Cal at a time when he was needy. In his youth he had been quite a physical specimen. We used to have a photograph of him lying on his back holding a board with a '49 Ford driving up on top of it. He had offers to play professional football and baseball and actually signed and went to spring training with the Pittsburgh Pirates, but he had to leave because he and his first wife had several small kids—in those days ballplayers did not make much money. How things have changed! He later had a stroke that disabled him and affected him financially. He was a guy who could do anything with his hands and, while he held a steady job, he always worked a second job.

Despite his vicious temper that I along with my mom and others were victims of, he had always taken care of Dale and had a generous side.

Now, instead of the new car he got every two years, his car was banged up and broken down. I spent hours restoring it for him as he worked by my side. He died soon afterward at only 59 years of age. During that season of his brokenness he came to Christ. His conversion was one of the most authentic I've witnessed. Watching that guy cry in the presence of the Lord was memorable. When I spoke at his funeral I sobbed. Here was a guy who had beaten my mom and me yet was really the only man who had been remotely a part of my life. The fact that there was such a genuine change in his life during the last few years probably added to my sense of loss. I remember his telling me how proud he was of me.

I didn't realize that there would never be a guy to help me along the way. I would be lying if I said I don't often wonder what it would have been like to have had someone, let alone a dad, who was interested in me and taught me how to be a man. When I see sons and daughters who reject their fathers—who are good men—it's beyond my comprehension. How blind can a son be (or a daughter for that matter) who disrespects a dad who is trying, when multitudes are crying out for a dad—someone who will root for them, pray for them, and pass his name on to them? The promise God gave us that He will return the hearts of the fathers to the children and the children's hearts to the fathers is something we are desperate for.

One day I got into an argument with Dale. During that fight my mom ran up with a plastic bat in her hand and began striking me in the face with it repeatedly. Somehow I froze while this was going on. Then I just turned around and ran. I walked about six miles to the Pennsylvania Turnpike wearing a short-sleeve shirt with two dollars in my pocket. It was an April evening and I was getting cold as the sun dipped down. I stuck out my thumb and a guy stopped and asked me where I was going. I replied simply, "Wherever you are."

Several days later I had managed to get to Miami Beach. This had not been without incident. On a lonely stretch in South Carolina, a guy in a blue Studebaker picked me up. I soon realized this guy was perverted. Eventually we pulled over at an old shack of a gas station and I made a run for it. He jumped into the car and started coming back around the access road as I ran for the main road. There were no other cars in sight. Then, as in a movie, a white Oldsmobile Cutlass came up over the horizon. I made it to the main road, got my thumb out, and he stopped—so did the guy driving the Studebaker as he was swinging onto the road from the gas station.

People often wonder what kids think during these times, maybe somehow expecting them to have a lucid moment and learn a lesson. The lesson I should have learned escaped me. At that age kids often are simply acting out of an instinct to survive. The innate desire to live, no matter how difficult it is, is still valuable and precious. This is important to know when working with people who have been abused or neglected. Most often they are reactors and not clear thinkers, and when they do make conclusions, many of those deductions are simply wrong. Rather than understanding that someone is trying to help them, they conclude that it's necessary to get them before they get you. This explains why those who have been abused ended up abusing others. The old saying that "hurt people hurt people" is a spiritual reality. John 20:23 (NKJV) says, "If you retain the sins of any, they are retained." I believe that if we understood what was being said here, we could comprehend why people end up being the very thing that they hate— abusers. They retain the sin in themselves.

That guy took me all the way to Miami. I believe God intervened in my life that day. I wonder if that perverted guy patrolled that lonely stretch of road. I wonder how many kids from shattered families disappear and are not even missed. Even then, I was aware that I had escaped, but I had no awareness of God. Think about it: I had escaped from a predator and was immediately picked up by a guy who fed me and took me about seven hundred miles—quite a change in circumstances. God had intervened! After a while the police in Florida caught me sleeping in a car and took me to a juvenile center. After a week of my giving them a false name, I finally caved in and told them who I really was. I was fourteen years old, so they shipped me back to Pittsburgh. My sister Debbie picked me up. I was pretty much on my own after that. Debbie would soon leave to move in with my aunt and uncle in Harrisburg, Pennsylvania, where she found a great job working for the auditor general at the state capitol. This was a great break for her. Aunt Lori and Uncle Joe were well off and took good care of her. Later in life after Uncle Joe died, Lori, the last sibling of my mother's family, was by herself. It was Debbie who rose to the occasion to take care of her and eventually moved her out to Indiana, where she would be in close proximity to her.

I always liked Aunt Lori and Uncle Joe; we would usually go to visit them during the summer. They never had children but had dogs and really good cars—Corvettes, Barracudas, Javelins—and they were also kind to my mother. One time when we had to separate as a family because we had nowhere to go, I went and stayed with them. They were living near Pittsburgh at the time. It's funny how little things stick out in your mind. I remember Lori asking me to get something from her car one day. When I came back, she gave me $5. It seemed like $1,000 at the time. I didn't expect anything; it certainly wasn't a family custom to give people money for doing things. For some reason I've always remembered that. I think that little act of kindness was somehow a seed of hope in my heart. Generosity can be a real tool to touch people's hearts. Often generosity really doesn't cost us much, and being generous with our praise, our encouragement, our time, our instruction, and our patience is so valuable. I think that when we get to heaven there will be some rewards we were expecting for some big things, but I think there are some little things where we obeyed the Holy Spirit that will result in a profound revelation and reward to us on that day.

Years later when my mom died, the funeral director called me and said

THE GOD OF INTERVENTIONS

my father had called him and asked if it was okay if he came to the funeral. We hadn't seen him in years and the slap to my brother's face was still unforgettable. Here I was, now a pastor with five children. I said, "Of course he can come." I told my children that he would be there. My oldest, Stacie, asked, "What do we call him?" I said, "Sir." By this time I had developed some compassion for him. When a man forgets his children and has never seen his grandchildren, he needs mercy. My kids lined up like little soldiers to meet him. They had never met a grandfather before. My wife, Penny's, dad had likewise left her mom for the lady down the street. Though my kids had grandmas, they never asked where their grandpas were. That's very interesting, and it shows how normal dysfunction can become.

Interestingly, at the end of his life I had a very strange encounter with my dad. My brother Lee called to say that our dad was in a nursing home. Albert was his name. When he and my mom ended their relationship, he had started a new family. He had two boys who were just a little younger than me. They had a good life. He was a successful building contractor, but he never gave my mom any financial support. His new wife owned the business, and though my mom had tried, she could never get a dime out of him. The laws are better today. It seems at the end of his life the other wife and kids were not around much, but my brother Lee had reached out to Albert and talked to him occasionally. I'm sure that, like me, he was still missing a dad and a man's voice and guidance.

I find it very interesting that my oldest son, who may have spent ten minutes with my father (I think he met him twice) is today a very successful building contractor. That trade seems to run in our family, with no connection to Albert. My youngest son is also very gifted in construction, and his skills are much in demand. Two of my sons-in-law are also in the building industry. Not only was my father a successful contractor, but four of his six brothers were contractors.

So when Lee told me that our dad was in the nursing home, I decided

I would go see him. I didn't tell Penny. It was a Saturday morning, and I told her I had a meeting. I was uncomfortable talking about it. I found him in the common room. Even in his broken-down state, I recognized him. I just went over and made small talk with him. I could tell there was some dementia there. Finally I said, "Do you know who I am?" He replied, "Sure—you're Keith." I was very surprised.

We talked some more. That was probably the most seriously I had ever talked to my dad. I won't tell you it made everything better. I went into his room and saw a photograph of him with his navy pals he had served with in World War II. I wondered how the war had affected him. I guess war affects people differently, just as our home life affected Lee and me differently. I was glad I had gone.

I believe if we are sensitive to the Holy Spirit, He will give us many opportunities to touch folks who may have done us harm and, in those acts of discomfort and awkwardness, He does a work in our lives that would be hard to duplicate.

Before I left I asked him if he was ready for heaven. That was why I had come. He answered with clarity that he was. When I asked how he knew, he said with clarity that he was trusting Jesus as his Lord and Savior. Who was I to argue? There was no religion in his family. At best, they were Catholics in name only. I believe my brother Lee was his lifeline. The quiet boy who got slapped across the face years before, who would go through a terrible injury in Vietnam and have a horrific first marriage, knew how to punch the devil in the face. I think I'll see my dad, Albert, in heaven (probably because of Lee)—hopefully with all my children and grandchildren.

After I came to salvation I went to see my mom. At this time she was drinking heavily and sitting in her apartment in the projects in the dark. Her blinds were down, probably in part to hide her appearance. She was always so conscious about how she looked. I used to think it was vanity. Now I understand that it was insecurity. Her first words to me were, "I heard you got religion." I tried to share with her, but it didn't go well.

By this time I had met Penny, who was and is the love of my life, and in her wisdom she had urged me to be tender. She herself had reached out and built a bridge with my mom. It took a few years, but eventually my mom, who lived under tremendous guilt, could finally believe that Jesus was not done with her. Well-meaning folks would make comments to her about my past life. It was hard for her to separate her failures and my successes. Her insecurities caused her a lot of pain; she once told me she wondered if people looked at her as that "terrible mother." I tried to assure her that this wasn't the case. Guilt is a paralyzing factor in many people's lives and we must be aware that it holds them back from walking in their full redemption. Making light of sin and failures does not alleviate guilt. Making much of Jesus and the cross will. I wish we could have gotten more time with her and had had the opportunity to care for her, although she did end up living with us for a short time. When I was a little boy I always told my mom that when I made my first $100 I would build her a house. Later on she reminded me of that. Unfortunately, I was never able to build her that house.

During the last ten years of her life we had a great relationship. She died at age 68 of lung cancer. We had been out of state for seven years planting churches and doing pro-life ministry in South Carolina and Florida. We were in the process of moving back to Pennsylvania when she died. I was traveling a lot during that time and could often swing my flights through Pittsburgh and spend a night with her. By then she was living in a low-income high-rise for seniors, which was much better than the projects. We would sit up late and talk. She loved old movies and knew all the actors—who was married to who and all that stuff. She would fuss over me and make the best sandwiches. Our relationship had been redeemed and we were able to make her life a little bit easier. Penny was a big part of that. She helped me navigate all my confusing, jumbled thoughts, knowing that it is always worthwhile to mend broken relationships when at all possible. When my kids saw "Grandma Graham Cracker," which they affectionately called her because she always had graham crackers, they had no clue of the bitter road we had traveled to get to where we were now. They had no clue that this little lady who was their grandma had herself endured such a devastating past. Even though we had a growing family, Penny insisted that we be generous and help my mom out.

It was during those late nights spent with my mom that I came to learn who this broken woman was as she shared some of her pain. She was very proud of me for my dedication to Penny and would remind me of it—I think in hopes of the family curse being broken. I also learned during one of those late nights that she had been pressured to abort me. Her marriage was on the rocks. She had physical problems and there was concern over me as well. The doctors told her a therapeutic abortion was no problem. When I asked her why she didn't do it, she just said, "Abortion was a dirty word then. It just didn't seem right!" It's still dirty to God! I can't help but think that thousands of abortions could have been avoided if society had continued to present the concept of abortion as "dirty" or just plain wrong! Thanks, Mom.

3

God Sends the "Kook Group"

Turtle Creek, Pennsylvania, is a small town of about 12,000, twenty miles east of Pittsburgh. It is home to the Vogues, the hit singing group of the sixties. It was also where David Wilkerson spent his teenage years. His dad was the pastor of the local Assembly of God church at the time. It no longer existed by the time I came along; the Christian and Missionary Alliance Church now possessed the property. Ironically years later when I was planting a church, we would use their building for special meetings before we owned our own property. Not only had I never heard of David Wilkerson, but to my knowledge I had never met a Christian. I never knew anyone who even attended church (except for a few uninterested Catholics).

Years later I met an older man, Bill Brehm, who was a world traveler. He spent much of his time in Africa in diamond exploration and diamond smuggling. He came to Christ when he heard Benson Idahosa present the gospel in open air meetings in Africa. Bill would have a big impact on my life. He was, from of all places, Turtle Creek, Pennsylvania, and had been a basketball star there.

Turtle Creek was next to East Pittsburgh, where I lived until the school merger. Those communities had little interaction. East Pittsburgh was a rougher area while Turtle Creek was the most average middle-class little town you can think of. It didn't have a project but did have a housing co-op which was a post-war housing strategy, in which low income families could buy in and not just rent. This was a significant sociological distinction and the atmosphere was far different. It was still inhabited by struggling families, but it was also populated by families who had done quite well but had decided to stay in the co-ops. This made it a stable community.

This is where I spent a lot of time as we congregated in large groups of around fifty to sixty. The police left us alone as we partied and carried on. I think their philosophy was "We know where they are." Most of the kids weren't bad and had intact families. Troublemakers from other groups stayed clear. Harper Drive had only one way in and one way out. Those driving in looking for trouble would get more than they bargained for. We could quickly close down the street, and they were trapped. That being said, by today's standards what we did was pretty calm. Although the police were content to let us party, some of the local residents saw the "problem" differently, or should I say an opportunity.

Enter here a group of women in their 40s and 50s. Eventually we would call them the "kook group," who had decided we were a captive audience and therefore they were going to evangelize us! If I had ever been witnessed to before, I don't remember it. To my knowledge none of the kids on that corner had any Christian background or understanding. The "kook group" consisted of four core members, but others tagged along at times. Jeannie and Joanne were definitely the ringleaders. We mocked them and were rude to them, but they just kept coming back. This lasted all summer. At some point they became part of the Friday and Saturday crowd. We would look for them and eventually they would come and we gave them begrudging respect. They were still weird but served as our weekend entertainment. They even started bringing guest speakers in. Ralph, an ex-motorcycle-type guy, came around with them. He was supposed to be the cool factor. We liked the ladies better, though, and the entertainment factor as they all talked together was sincere if nothing else.

I remember one morning getting a knock on my car window. It was Ernie, Jeannie's husband. He was not part of the "kook group" and just rolled his eyes at it all. Our gathering spot was just across the street from his home. This day Jeannie sent him out to get me for breakfast. As she served me eggs and toast, she told me that the Lord had given her a song. Of course, I had no clue of what she was talking about. I pictured sheet music floating out of heaven. She then proceeded to belt out a song in her operatic voice. I sat stunned. This was weird. Ernie rolled his eyes. The eggs were good but in no time I was out of there!

These ladies often talked about God and how He spoke to them. They also spoke another language they called "tongues." They would pray for us and they seemed to know things about us that we had never revealed. Not long before, they had been a Catholic prayer group but then they started hanging around an Assembly of God church in Trafford, several towns away. They received the baptism of the Holy Spirit and spoke in tongues. They were now turbo-charged Christians and, as the scripture tells us, they received boldness to witness. If you have a hard time with that, you'll have to take it up with God. I had nothing to do with it but the evidence and the fruit were pretty clear. I like to say that they decided to start street preaching before someone could talk them out of it. The personal indwelling power of the Holy Spirit is essential to holy living and holy actions. One reason many churches are not seeing a spiritual breakthrough is that so few of their people have been baptized in the Holy Spirit.

The "kook group" had been at it all summer. They had expanded their efforts by inviting us over to Joanne's for food. We had become friends. We knew they were trying to help—we just thought they were weird. Their lives were by no means shining examples of the "great American dream." Jeannie's son had crippling muscular dystrophy. Her husband was not into

Jesus. Joanne's husband had died suddenly when he was young. One of the other ladies had a husband who was rumored to be violent and abusive with her. This was not exactly a great sales pitch.

At this point I really wasn't a believer in God. I could not understand how, if what they were saying was true, I had gone through life up to this point and had had no one else share this gospel with me or my family—not even invite us to church. That seemed to be proof, if nothing else, that God did not exist. Something else, however, started to happen in the middle of all this: I was approached by strangers who witnessed to me about Jesus. On one occasion I picked up a hitchhiker who told me about Jesus. All my life no one had spoken to me of Jesus, and now I was hearing about Him from several different folks. Why was this happening all of a sudden? They weren't just preaching—they were praying. It got to the point at which I was expecting someone to witness to me. I even asked the "kook group" if they had set me up. Of course, with that question they were cackling and praising the Lord. In addition to the street church they were trying to run, they were praying for us by name. We were not aware of it at the time, however.

I remember vividly the night I finally had had enough of all this God stuff. I had tried to believe and had given all the effort I could to figure it out, although I was often high and or drunk during their sermons. I finally blurted out, "I wish I could believe all this stuff you're talking about—'new birth,' 'new creation,' 'new mercies,' 'new life'!" I guess I was absorbing something. Jeannie's answer was short and with authority, and it has always stuck with me. She quoted Ephesians 2:8–10 and simply said, "Tucci, if you're sincere He will give you the faith to believe." There were several of us around, but I said with my eyes open, "God, if You're who they say You are, here I am." It wasn't as arrogant as it sounds. The prospect of a new life was simply beyond anything I could believe, no matter where it was coming from. For about a week I felt as if I were in a birth canal. For the first time in my life I felt conviction over sin. I remember several days after my prayer looking in the mirror asking myself out loud if I was losing my mind. I began passing up opportunities to sin. Something was happening.

CHAPTER

4

God's Mafia

"Let's go to church!" After about a week of soul torment, a peace began coming over me. I had never experienced peace! The rage and anger were leaving me as I was experiencing something I could not explain. When I would ask questions or try to explain it to the "kook group," they would resort to their cackling and praising the Lord. They were aware that the "hound of heaven" was on my trail. I didn't presume to call myself a Christian or to say I was forgiven, but I was awakened.

I began seeing my life from a different perspective, tasting hope—and it was amazing. So I said to Joanne and Jeannie, "Shouldn't I go to church or something?" Of course, they thought that was a great idea, which generated more of their rejoicing, almost as if I weren't there. There was a problem, however, that I was unaware of. They were still Catholics to some degree. They knew they could not take me to the Catholic church, so off to Christian Life Church (an Assembly of God church in Trafford, Pennsylvania) we went. As it turned out, they never went back to the Catholic church.

My first Sunday at church was memorable. It began with two big guys hugging me at the front door, causing me to pivot and head back out until a hand grabbed my shoulder, something like "God's mafia." It was George

Woods. He had seen what was happening and jumped in. He started calling me "Brother," saying, "Brother this" and "Brother that." George was in his fifties, was a successful businessman, and would later come to visit me at Bible school, take me out to lunch with a couple of other students, put a twenty-dollar bill in my pocket, and encourage me. This really was a new life.

When the people started singing, it was loud and everyone belted out singing, "This is the day that the Lord has made." It seemed as if they sang it fifty times. I don't know that I opened my mouth, though. This was all new to me—I did wonder if they knew any other songs. Then, just as suddenly, they moved on to another. I would learn later that not all churches were like this one. Just as soon as I was getting acclimated to the singing, the lady in front of me belted out a message in tongues and then fell straight back, whacking her head on the pew and just lay there. This didn't seem to bother anyone but me. I could not understand why the holy people around her were not concerned. I leaned over the pew and looked. All of a sudden there was an interpretation of tongues coming from across the room; just as this lady had spoken in an unknown tongue, someone gave the interpretation. I didn't know a lot, but I knew this wasn't natural—it was supernatural. I didn't know that the Bible said that tongues are a sign—not to the believer but to the unbeliever. To think that many churches have shut down the Holy Spirit to appeal to unbelievers is a problem; appealing to them and bringing the presence of God do not have to be mutually exclusive. The songs started again. The well-dressed lady eventually made it up off the floor (with no help from anyone), straightened herself out, and acted as if nothing had happened. She would have fit in great with the "kook group." No one seemed concerned, so why should I be?

Soon the preacher began. He was a man of about 60 with a full head of silver hair and a sharp suit. As he preached I felt as if the "kook group" had conspired with him and that he was talking to me. He was a forceful speaker who would get very red in the face, which contrasted greatly with his silver hair. They called him "Rev"—and revved up he was! Then he gave the altar call. Before I knew what was happening, I was up there on my knees. Tears began flowing, tears I didn't know I had. I didn't know why they came—they just kept coming. It's hard to describe what was going on, and I certainly didn't understand. I didn't know being saved involved this upheaval of my gut; it was as if I were puking out the world. I guess I imagined following Jesus was more about making a mental decision to the facts—the real facts of life. I thought the new life was a new way of thinking. I didn't know I would actually get a genuinely new life. The Holy Spirit had promised that out of our bellies would flow living water—right now He was drilling a well. As powerful a conversion experience as I had, it's critical that we understand that experiences don't save us. Rather, faith built on God's Word saves us. It may sound odd, but I don't trust experiences. Many people seem to have experiences and never possess what God intended for them.

To this day I'm able to just melt in the presence of God. Sometimes when I'm preaching it's all I can do to keep from weeping, and sometimes I can't hold back. It was as if God were showing me there was something else in me. I don't remember crying before that for years. I'm sure that as a little boy I had. I remember when my grandfather died—being at the gravesite and seeing my mom cry, I started crying too. I would have been in second grade then. He was someone I really didn't know. My grandmother ruled that roost and barked orders at him, and he escaped daily from her to the bar on the corner. I think my mom identified with him as someone also being beat down by her mom. I don't remember crying after that, although I'm sure there were times I wanted to. I don't think I knew how.

I told some of my friends what had happened. No one mocked me; most of them just shrugged their shoulders. A couple of them just told me I was tripping, that the LSD and mescaline had gotten to me. I can just imagine some of the conversations they must have had. They knew I had never been religious and still wasn't. Now I didn't want to party and had a hunger to read the Bible. There's no doubt that some of them thought it was a fad that would fade away and told me so. The truth is that my use of those strong hallucinogens was a reasonable assumption to these guys who had never witnessed a genuine conversion.

CHAPTER

5

The "Rev"

My life began rotating in a different direction. It seemed as though I saw Jeannie or Joanne almost every day. Often I would show up to hang out with the old gang but got bored and slipped away. I was now reading a Bible the ladies had gotten for me. The amazing part was not all the things I didn't understand but rather the fact that I could understand anything at all. I could see the same Jesus they had told me about and He looked just the way they said He did. Each Sunday we went to church. For weeks I answered the altar call—most often crying. A lot of the time I wasn't even sure why I was crying. I was being cleansed. The Holy Spirit was softening me as I humbled myself to repent to Him. He used this to develop my spiritual sensitivity and awareness.

I began to realize that a lot of my friends had previously been careful not to cross me for fear of retribution; they realized my unmetered response was not worth the hassle. Once in eleventh grade my English teacher played a record in class about "getting in touch with yourself." It was some kind of psychological babble. At the end she started asking various kids what they would do if they knew they were going to die. For some reason she called on me. I said I would make a list of everyone I wanted to get even with, then follow through with it. That threw a wet blanket on the class, but it pretty much summarizes how I was going through life—surviving at best. Now, with my eyes open, the reflections I began having about myself were not a pretty picture. Because of all the craziness in our lives, I had no real reference point.

Today when I try to convince church people who are engaging unchurched folks or discipling new converts about the lack of a reference point, it's difficult for them to grasp and it's difficult to explain, but being literally lost is the best way to describe it. I was wandering through life—more accurately barreling through, completely out of touch with how close I was to the edge. I was lost. Today much of our world is lost in every sense of the word. We must not assume that they have a moral or even philosophical starting point; they have no awareness of absolute truth, no clear understanding of right or wrong. We try defining God by our own intellect and life as opposed to seeing that we are made in God's image. We must be dependent on Scripture and not on our own wit and wisdom to disciple them.

I was voted by my senior class as most likely to die. This was not because I was courageous but because I was clueless. My friends were now clueless about what was happening to me, but the good old "kook group" seemed to have a grasp on it. They just kept praising the Lord. During this time I had a lot of questions about the Bible—not just about what it said but why I should trust it. The "kook group" was not completely prepared to give me the answers that I needed, but they had friends. I learned about the Dead Sea Scrolls, fulfilled prophecy, archaeology, and other scientific facts.

Years later I led a pro-life outreach in the San Francisco area. The first American showing of the Dead Sea Scrolls was on exhibit. I stood in line to see part of the book of Isaiah. It was amazing. Josh McDowell's book *Evidence That Demands a Verdict* had a big impact on me regarding the authority of Scripture. It seemed that for every truth I came across, a conflict was produced. I had already wrestled about whether Jesus was real and divine. Why did His followers never tell me or my family? Now as I was seeing the Bible as God's Word, how was it that so few knew this? How could I be going to this terrific church and everyone outside the church not even know who the pastor, "Rev," was?

By this time I was confident in my salvation. Ephesians 2:8–10 (ESV) was my foundation:

> For by grace you have been saved through faith. And this is not your own doing; it is the gift of God, not a result of works, so that no one may boast. For we are his workmanship, created in Christ Jesus for good works, which God prepared beforehand, that we should walk in them.

Even though I was having very interesting experiences, I had been taught well to live by what God said, not what I felt. The whole feeling thing was quite a roller coaster, but I was rolling in the right direction. Now I was going to church three times a week. I was not partying, drinking, or doing street life. I just didn't want to. It was boring. I even learned to drink coffee. The "kook group" had a whole network of prayer meetings and Bible studies. I met some amazing people. Where had these people been all my life?

I was working at UPS loading trucks, starting each day 4:15 a.m. Amazingly, I was sober every day and able to be there. It was really cool—a guy who ran his own "kook group" was there. He was my age but was way beyond me spiritually. During our breaks we would go out and sit in my car and do Bible studies. It was hard for me to believe that he didn't know my "kook group." He was just like them. I had heard of the baptism of the Holy Spirit and witnessed people speaking in tongues. I had tried to receive this experience, but it wasn't happening. One day in the car he did a sneak attack on me, reached over, and laid hands on me. I received!

I was happy just to be saved and enjoyed the people who were "holier" than me, content just to eat the crumbs off the table. In a word, I was grateful. To this day I thank God every day for my salvation. When I received the baptism of the Holy Spirit, I felt like a son. Somehow I understood God and the equality of His grace in His people. Later this would become more significant when the realization of His calling came upon my life. It empowered me to cling to His calling and not my qualifications. He doesn't call the qualified—otherwise none would be called; instead, He qualifies the called. Paul wrote in Galatians 1:15 that he was called from the time he was in his mother's womb. In 1 Timothy 1:12 he wrote, "I thank Christ Jesus our Lord, who hath enabled me, for that he counted me faithful, putting me into the ministry." These two contrasting principles reveal the glory and grace of His calling and the stewardship of our diligence.

I don't think I had ever really admired anybody, except maybe Roberto Clemente, the starting right fielder for the Pittsburgh Pirates. As a kid I hid myself in baseball. I had a little transistor radio that I would go to bed with and listen to their night games. Bob Prince was the announcer and his voice would comfort me. He was the ultimate home team guy, always defending his team and his boys. Years later when they fired him, I was sad. I felt as though I had lost a friend.

I often left the house in the summer and on weekends to play baseball and not come home until it was too dark to continue playing. Sometimes in the projects we would play "strike out" between the buildings, looking for a place where there were no parked cars or maybe just a few junkers. The buildings were about one hundred feet apart. One guy would bat, and we would paint or draw a strike zone on the wall. Every pitch outside the strike zone was counted as a walk; inside the strike zone it was an out. A swing and a miss were an out. If the ball hit the other wall above a certain line, it was a homer. Ground balls that got past the pitcher were singles. We would play with two guys. If we had a third, he would play the field and face the winner. If we had four, we could have two teams. We played for hours and start all over the next day, stopping only if we lost a ball. That was a tragedy. Balls were hard to come by. Of course, I was always "Roberto" when I was up to bat. I still enjoy baseball. Clemente died tragically when his small plane crashed during a trip in 1972 to take relief to earthquake victims in Nicaragua.

Now let me tell you about "Rev." His real name was Paul Ridings, an evangelist who happened to be a pastor and was tough and fun. He had a way with men. When he would preach he would say, "Mister," and every guy in the place knew he was talking to them. He had taken the Gospel Tabernacle from fifty folks in a storefront to a new building at a prominent intersection. The congregation was now about three hundred people. Many of them were upper-class businesspeople. Some were old-timers who had made the transition. Some were young families, and there were a few like me. A few years later I ended up serving as the associate pastor there in between planting churches. If you had told me or most anyone that this would have happened, they would have thought it was a joke, except of course the "kook group."

This is the first time in my life that I really looked up to a man and would hang out at his house with his kids and run errands with him and for him. It just seemed logical that I should follow in his footsteps. The "kook group" informed me that I was "called." I wasn't sure what that meant, but it sounded better than being left behind. There were other young people going off to Bible school to exciting places like Springfield, Missouri; Tulsa, Oklahoma; and Minneapolis. When I asked Rev about Bible school, to his credit he didn't throw water on it. To this day, I'm not sure if it was the right thing, time, or place, but Jesus is the Redeemer and here I am, many years later. He told me about a little school in Butler, Pennsylvania.

There the pastor of the Butler Assembly of God had started a full-time school and now had about five faculty members and fifty students. My class would boost the attendance to seventy-plus students. I guess Rev wrote a letter and they took me in at the last minute. I really didn't have any money. At the time, I was living with my sister and her husband, Steve. She and my brother Lee had both given their lives to Jesus.

Looking back to how Lee had come to Christ, one day a group of guys were meeting in the parking lot of the Ponderosa Restaurant, which was right behind the mobile home park that Lee lived in. He passed them as he walked to the bus. They spoke to him and tried to engage him. Lee had always had an attraction to dark things as a kid. He read things about witchcraft and loved watching horror films. A guy I knew from high school told me he paid Lee for a love potion to cast a spell on a girl so that she would like him! At this point in his life, Lee had survived his Vietnam experience with a severely mangled leg that required a built-up shoe. These guys took an interest in him and began praying.

As they witnessed to him, he snarled at them and cursed. Like the "kook group," however, they were persistent. Soon he began conversing with them and eventually came to Christ just weeks after me without any correspondence between us. By the time I had reached out to him, the Holy Spirit had beat me to it. Although he had a rough ride through a bad marriage, he joined me in Bible school and actually finished at that school (while I didn't). Lee never served as a lead pastor or paid staff anywhere, but he has remained faithful to the Lord. He served in his church and cared for those in need. Today he ministers to shut-ins and is a trophy of God's grace. He's still quiet and reserved but is totally a follower of Jesus.

My introduction to Bible school was a culture shock. I expected the same exuberance there that I had experienced at Christian Life Church. Instead, I was met with a somber type of atmosphere. This is not to say that there were not people there who had joy. Most of the students came from middle-class families and were well educated. Many could play a musical instrument. Several of them were from pastors' families. There was also a group like me, who came from broken and unchurched homes. Jim, my roommate, was one of them.

I was never good in a classroom. Being in all those different schools growing up had convinced me that I was pretty stupid. The effect that changing schools and uninterested teachers have on a child's emotional and intellectual ability is hard to understand for others who have never been in that scenario. I wonder how many people we are ministering to who have been deeply affected by this type of trauma. The gift of encouragement and affirmation is so critical in discipleship. I mostly passed—in spite of my grades, not because of them. Somehow I had learned how to read and actually liked to read. That had been a saving grace. It enabled me to read the Bible, then read on my own in Bible school to catch up with the class, because I could not keep up in the classroom. I had quit school so many times in tenth and eleventh grade that the principal, little Ozzie Rometo, (who we called the "Bug") told me that I should just not come back, that if I wanted to quit, I didn't need to notify him or anyone else. During my senior year I needed an English credit to pass. The problem was that the English teacher, Mrs. Bush, refused to have me in her class because of my behavior. Ozzie told me he would pass me if I promised not to come back. To this day, I have no clue as to what motivated me to even be interested in going back to school to graduate.

Those were my academic credentials. In my younger years teachers routinely called me out in front of the class. In those days it seemed that all the teachers would read the test scores out loud. Mine was almost always the worst. When I knew they were working their way down the alphabet, with the last name Tucci, I was always near the end—which only prolonged the agony and torture of the embarrassment that I knew was to come. I would try to pretend that I was doing something on my desk. If the boys snickered, I could smack them at recess, but when the girls did, it just hurt.

I hated going to school in those elementary school days. Every day was painful. Lunchtime was also embarrassing when I really didn't have anything I had brought to eat. I learned to move around and go to the bathroom so that kids would not notice. Sometimes when they did, I would tell them elaborate lies about why I didn't have lunch or had undesirable items for lunch. It took me a while to realize that they knew I was lying and that they were playing me. It's sad to me that during those years how disinterested my teachers were. I had a fifth-grade teacher who would mock me and show the other kids my poor work. I'm sure not all teachers were like this, but I was unfortunate in that I don't have very many fond memories of teachers who tried to help me, let alone show specific concern.

In sixth grade I got a break. Our two sixth-grade teachers were big sports fans. So our classes were pitted against each other in gym competition in every team sport. We had moved again, now living in a nice home in a middle-class neighborhood because Mom had remarried. I was an unknown commodity in the new school. It was clear that I played with a fury that these suburban kids had never seen, and I emerged as the top athlete. Mr. Weaver encouraged that, and I fed on that encouragement. It had been hard to play team sports up until then because of moving around. Now I had a little confidence and he never humiliated me in the classroom.

We did have an incident in which I got my foot caught in the cyclone fence and it ripped my shoe and cut my foot. I flipped out. My mom was heading to another divorce, and there was a lot of fighting about money. I started screaming about how much the shoe cost and, trust me, they were Kmart specials—nothing fancy. The teachers had to restrain me. I remember it because it was me who embarrassed myself, not someone else. Fortunately, it was close to the end of the school year so I didn't have to deal with it for very long. By September we were gone, and I lived with Cal, Dale's dad, for the start of seventh grade.

Now I was sitting in Bible school with students who knew a lot of this stuff offhand. Every day was work. I had thought it would be church all day long. An incident happened in Bible school that's better than fiction. Our music teacher and her husband were from Wales and very sophisticated, educated, and accomplished. He was the pastor of a nearby church. As I said, many of the students were accomplished musicians, so our class moved fast. I was lost and had given up asking questions. She could not comprehend the questions I would ask because they were so beneath her, let alone trying to instruct me. In addition to that, I sing badly. I'm the joyful noise guy, completely tone deaf—a musical nightmare. Choir was part of the class and of course, I was throwing everyone off.

We all had student mailboxes in which staff and professors would return papers and leave instructions. These, of course, were pre-computer days. One day I got a note that the disciplinary committee wanted to see me. I knew this was not good news and I was shaken up. These were holy people I had to go before. When I went in to see them, I was scared. I had heard that the last guy in there had been asked to leave school. The president of the school informed me that one of the professors had filed a charge against me. To say I was mortified would be an understatement. I asked what it was. They told me that our music teacher had accused me of insubordination. Embarrassingly, I didn't even know what *insubordination* meant—I had to have them tell me. They told me that she said I was intentionally disrupting her class by singing so badly during choir practice as to throw everybody off. You can't make this stuff up. I just blurted out, "I'm that bad! Honest—I'm really that bad!"

The president was a kind man who had picked me up hitchhiking from work one evening, and we had enjoyed a great conversation. I think he had a soft spot for me. He said, "Why don't you leave the room for a minute?" I surmise that he then explained my situation to the other professors. They called me back and told me to go to class and work hard. Several days later in music class the teacher walked right up to me and said, "You may have fooled them, but you're not fooling me. You're going to stand here in the choir and you're going to move your mouth, but I don't want one sound coming out."

That year school wasn't all bad. My grades were not good and I barely passed. I had to work hard to keep up because I was also holding down a job. Fortunately, I did learn some good study habits. I very much appreciated some of the kids who had been raised in great homes and great churches who became friends of mine. At the end of year when I left Bible school, I knew I would not be coming back—it was obvious to me that being a pastor was something that was not in my future. As I compared myself to the others, it was clear that I lacked most of what they had in every category. That appraisal was probably factually accurate, but, as I would learn, God calls a person and then does the qualifying.

My plan was very simple. I was going to go back to my home church and be the best church member anybody could have. It was my home and it was the best place I had ever been in my life. These are the people who loved me, cared about me, believed in me, and encouraged me. I was going home.

CHAPTER

6

Learning to Follow the Leader

I wasn't really concerned about what I was going to do for a living. As odd as it may seem, I had never been concerned about that. I had made a startling conclusion growing up in the projects—if you didn't want to be poor, you had to get a job. I can remember as a young boy watching people come and go from the projects. Some people would come through hard times—maybe divorce, a death in the family, or even the loss of a job. I would watch some of them for a year or two or three and they would work their way out. Often they didn't have great jobs, but they did have jobs.

When my mom was sober she worked hard. She scrubbed people's floors, she waited on tables, she did anything she could. I don't think we should shame folks who need help, but in our efforts to help them, it should be an intervention of help as opposed to a lifestyle of intervention. In those days we received food stamps—brightly-colored coupons that did not allow you to purchase alcohol, tobacco, or any other non-necessity. Many folks sold those stamps for less than their face value. Today most states issue debit cards for people to randomly spend money, which in many cases only prolongs the problem.

From the time I was a young boy, I would knock on people's doors and ask them for returnable pop bottles that you got two cents apiece for. Folks would often stockpile them, because it was a hassle to drag them back to the store. I would gather them up and take them back to the store. I would knock on doors and ask if I could wash people's cars. In spite of my many character flaws, I was never lazy. I actually enjoyed working. I think I saw it as a way out.

Now I have to tell you that not all my work was honest. Even as a full-blown heathen, I was at least industrious. As younger kids, we would steal the copper gutters and downpipes off government buildings and take them to the junkyard to sell for pennies on the dollar. One time when the authorities were on to us, they were coming to my house to find my stash, but I got tipped off ahead of time. I was able to hide everything. We got a little more sophisticated as time went on and went into the midnight auto parts business, stealing car stereos, tires, and wheels. People would tell us what they needed and we would go out and find it. Later on we came up with an even better plan. We would call local wrecking yards and tell them that we needed certain parts for cars. They would take those parts off and have them ready for pickup in the junkyard. We would show up at night, climb over the fence, grab the part, and make a profit. Of course, you had to be careful not to do this too regularly or they would catch on to you. At one junkyard we figured out that they had no security on Sundays. So we would take orders from people who needed parts—fenders, doors, seats, even transmissions (engines were too heavy). We would go to the junkyard and work for hours dismantling parts and be out of there before it was dark.

After I got saved I used my knowledge more redemptively and would visit small used car lots and ask what work they may need done on some of their cars. These guys would take a chance on a kid with a toolbox and allow me to prove myself on a low-priced car. I actually did pretty well. I was doing this as Penny and I prepared to marry. In addition to that, sometimes folks would be looking for a car. I would find them that car, negotiate the price, and make a commission. I would also buy cars and sell them. I found out really quickly that Mustangs and Camaros were very easy to resell. It didn't matter what condition they were in—people would buy them. My plan was simple: I would come back, get a job, make myself available to serve in the church, and do whatever I could to help.

I had met Penny before, but I didn't know her very well. The next summer our worship leader decided he was taking a group of young people on a choir tour. Penny was on that tour. Obviously, because of my musical background, I did not qualify. But I did know how to drive a van. So I went along and drove. During that time Penny and I got to know each other. I was, of course, very attracted to her—she was a looker. But I also watched how tender she was with other people and how well she related with older folks. I liked her intellect as well. She was obviously very smart and was working as a legal secretary at the time. Had she not become the mother of eight children and been willing to move and travel with her whole brood, I believe she would have been a great lawyer or anything else God had put in her heart. She gave that up for me and saw value in what we were doing together. Soon I was convinced that she was the girl for me! I did everything I could to win her. I was still wild and rough around the edges, but most of my wildness was kingdom stuff, doing crazy things for Jesus.

Often on Sunday afternoons I would get a stack of New Testaments. If I couldn't talk somebody into going with me, I would go alone to the local hospital. I would just wander the halls, sticking my head into the rooms where there were people by themselves. I would go in and share the gospel with them and offer to pray with them. I remember one older man who was very bitter. He finally agreed to let me pray for him, and as I went to leave, I gave him a New Testament. He asked me how much it would cost and I said it didn't cost anything. He began to argue with me and say, "I know you're up to something. Nobody has ever given me anything in my whole life." That always stuck with me. As I shared the gospel again with him, he began weeping, and I was able to pray with him.

I was plugged into our church and wasn't completely bummed out about the revelation that I would never be a pastor (or so I thought). I realized that God could give me other ways to serve and I wanted to serve my pastor and the Lord as best I could. I was learning to follow the leading of the Holy Spirit. I was not always aware of it at the time, but those lessons were invaluable later in life.

One of the first things I did when I got home from Bible school was to call him. His wife told me he was down at the church. It was a Saturday and he was cleaning the church. Even though we had a growing church, he augmented his pastor's salary by serving as the janitor, if you can believe that! They paid him a separate salary. Thank God—the leaders in the church got a better revelation and eventually took care of him in a more generous way. He was in there wiping down the pews with furniture polish. I told him I was home and I was there to serve in any way I could. We hung out for a while and he said, "Let's go get some lunch." That became a weekly ritual. I would go down to the church, he would be there cleaning, and then pretty soon he would drift off and I would finish the cleaning. Sometimes I would pull his car into the carport and wash it for him. Then we would go to lunch. Often I would head home with him. I'm sure there were times that I was under their feet. I always tell people that he discipled me by accident. He was not an easy guy to get close to. Although we were a generation apart, his story was somewhat similar to mine in that he was not a church kid. He got saved during the war, went to Bible school, and then moved right into ministry. He never really had a pastor or any guys around him to help him.

His relationship with me was unique. In the church culture he was trained in, you were taught not to get close to folks, so what was happening with us was most likely beyond his comfort zone. As time goes on, I appreciate those times even more and am thankful for those great memories. They were vital and key for me. He was a very direct guy—and I needed that! He could also be abrupt and rough, which pushed people away at times, but that was not a big deal to me. I was accustomed to rough talk. Amazingly I comprehended that my serving him on Saturday mornings was empowering him in ministry. I think those times became meaningful for him as well. The negative side was that because I esteemed him so much, I also emulated him, and as a result, I justified being gruff at times. I was his chief defender in those matters when others got offended. My picture of a spiritual guy was not one who was meek but someone who let the chips fall where they would—that's certainly not to say that reflected his heart or motive.

The truth is, our church had very little revelation about discipleship and one-on-one ministry. Those Saturdays spent asking him questions and hearing him share his life with me were incredible. I remember one day he said to me, "Run up to the house and tell Edith to give you a tie. We're going to go to the hospital." That day he took me with him and demonstrated how to make a hospital call. He showed me how to walk into the hospital room, introduce myself as a minister, and offer to pray. He was such a great evangelist. I can tell you, I've had times later as a pastor when I would go into the hospital and offer to pray for someone and the person in the next bed would ask me to pray for him or her too. God would start to move and I would get called from room to room being asked to pray for people. It's happened more than once. Often ministry is right there for us while we're waiting for something bigger or something better.

Jesus often talked about having our eyes and ears opened. He taught a parable in which a man went to where men were looking for work and hired them. Finally at the end of the day he asked those who were still idle why they were there. Their answer should challenge anyone who is *waiting* to be used by God: "No man has hired me." Maybe we're waiting to get behind a pulpit thinking that somehow that's where ministry starts. John Wesley said that the world was his parish and I think people should be our pulpits. If you've ever been in a trauma/ICU waiting room late at night and looked into the eyes of the desperate faces, you would understand what I mean—ministry opportunities are all around us.

By the time the next year came around, Penny and I were talking seriously about getting married and she asked me, "What about ministry?" I told her I was just not sure. She encouraged me to go back to school. Remember: we really didn't have a mechanism for raising up ministers, so school was our only option. So we made a radical decision with no money—we were going to get married that fall and then leave immediately to go back to Bible school. This time I was going to go to a different school, Rhema Bible Training Center, in Tulsa, Oklahoma, where some other people from our church had gone and seemed to have had a better experience. I needed a fresh chance if this were going to work. I have often wondered since then what would have happened if Penny had not asked me that question. I think of the risk she was taking—leaving her mom, her job, working while I went to school, with no friends of family, no dad to look out for her.

I did get a job while going to school as a janitor working the 3:00-to-midnight shift. She would get home from her job as a legal secretary in a prestigious law firm in Tulsa, bring me dinner, and hang out with me. That's how we got to see each other. The other folks we worked with were good with this, but soon the supervisor told me that Penny could not visit me at work anymore. I had to find a job where I could still spend time with her. Fortunately that worked out. We had gotten married that August and several days later we headed for Tulsa. Let me tell you about the "Blessing Mobile," our car's pet name, during part of this time.

I had become good friends with a young single guy, Dan, in the church, who was a very positive influence on me. He had lost his job in sales and was out of work for a little while. Then he was offered a very good job. One day in prayer I felt the Lord speaking to me: "Somebody's going to come to you and ask for a financial favor." Now that had to be God because I really didn't have any money. Penny and I maybe had $1,000 saved heading into marriage. Dan told me he had been offered a great job, but the condition was that he had to have a car. Because he had been out of work for a few months, he couldn't get the financing. He asked me if I would cosign something. I never would have done that otherwise and I don't recommend it to anyone, but I knew the Lord had spoken to me. I understood that if he didn't make the payments, it was my problem. So I talked to Penny about it and agreed to do it.

He told me he had the car picked out, a Pontiac Catalina, at a dealership. I went up and looked at it and then saw another one that I liked better. It had more equipment and was a different color (which I preferred). I negotiated the price down to a better deal than he had gotten on the other car, and I bought it. I put it in my name only, skipping the whole co-signing thing and understanding that the responsibility for the car payments was totally on me. He was surprised but quite happy with the deal I had made. His job went very well and eight months later, as Penny and I were preparing to get married, he said to me, "If you want to take the car, just take it and pick up the payments." He had put money down on it and just wanted to be a blessing to us. The thought of having a car payment on the verge of getting married and going to school was something that was a bit out of my faith zone. However, Penny said, "I believe God wants us to have the car. I think we can do it." We drove that car 200,000 miles and hardly put a nickel into it. Every couple of months somebody would bang into it and we got an insurance check. The car more than paid for itself in its lifetime. As mentioned before, we called it the "Blessing Mobile."

I finally gave it away to a guy in the church who needed the transmission out of it. That car was supernaturally blessed. We had it for a number of years and literally collected more money on it than we had ever paid for it. After an accident I would be pounding out dents or buying used fenders and doors and saving us a bunch of money. At one point I had the car completely repainted and it was like brand new. Again, this was one of those little signs that God used to show me the depth of Penny's spirituality and her willingness to trust God and trust me to take care of us.

The next year of college was very positive. I was stirred deeply in my being and was convinced that I was called into ministry again. I had stopped comparing myself to others and was now free to really consider what the Lord might have for us. I wasn't so sure about pastoral ministry, but I had definitely moved into a new place. Comparing yourself to others either deflates or puffs you up. We need to be stewards of the grace of God of our own calling and talents and not compare our abilities with those of others.

Jesus told a parable about handing out talents. Three guys got three different amounts—no excuses, no reasons. I just came to the place that I didn't have to be a five-talent guy but needed to invest what I did have. An opportunity came up with a small group of people looking for a pastor. Actually there were several opportunities. I prayed and asked what direction I should go and said, "Lord, I'm going to go and do this. I'm going to see if these people will have me. If this is You, I'm ready to go; if it's not, it's okay—we'll just go back home again and be the best pastor's helpers in the world. I'll get a job. I'll start a business. I'll go to the mission field. I'll preach in the jails. I'll disciple new believers. I'll clean the church. I really don't care"—and I really didn't. As it turned out, this group of about fourteen people decided that this 22-year-old guy who was just wet behind the ears was going to be their pastor of their church, Cadogan Union Church, in a little town about an hour from our home church in Trafford.

After a couple of months of ministry, God moved. Ray was on his deathbed. They had called the undertaker to come to the hospital to get his body. He was in a coma. He didn't even know me. I was there because his neighbor had asked me to go and pray. I sat through the whole night beside him, praying in tongues. In the morning Ray woke up—a surprise to everybody. The undertaker was actually in the ICU to check on his status; his hearse was backed up in the hospital loading dock. Ray testified that he heard everything that was happening while he was in the coma and that he had gotten saved—while in the coma. He had also heard his brothers fighting about some of his possessions! Ray became a sign and wonder. Many people in that small town came to Christ.

Now the church began growing, but after about a year I realized I was in over my head. I often explain to people that I had told them everything I knew. I told them twice—then I made some stuff up. This is not far from the truth. I realized, even at that young age, that I had to get somebody to come there to handle the church. My plan was just to go back home to Christian Life Church and see what the Lord was going to do, and that's what we did. We had some other offers to go and do some ministry, but I kept myself busy serving in my home church. During this time I also began systematically visiting the local county jail and state prison. The church leadership of Christian Life (our home church) asked me if I would join the staff. We were still a growing church. We had a youth pastor, a music pastor, a senior pastor, and I would be the associate pastor.

CHAPTER

7

The God Who Troubles Your Waters

We were doing great. I was on staff. Penny was working for a local Christian television station. Rev had me preaching on a regular basis. I was introducing discipleship into our church. However, there was a problem. Edith, Rev's wife, was not herself. Someone once described her as the lady who looked as if she had swallowed a light bulb. She played the piano, played the organ, knew everyone's names, and organized kids' events. Her gifts would be intimidating to most folks. She was always kind to me and often set an extra plate for me at the table.

She had begun limping a bit and then her beautiful speech began to slur. We were all concerned and praying while the doctors were not able to figure it out. Finally she visited a specialist and we were told a diagnosis was coming. I distinctly remember the day that Rev was waiting for the call. All of our offices were lined up next to each other. The secretary's, Dee's, office was first, then the youth pastor's, Steve's, office, then the worship pastor's, Jim's, office, then mine, and then Rev's. We had the phones with light-up buttons. You could hear each call come in, then knew who it was for depending on which light was illuminated.

Then came the call for Rev. He was expecting it. We were all expecting it. I was in my office. My door was half open, which was kind of my custom. In a few minutes came a light knock on my door. It was Rev. He said, "Can I come in?" He was not a guy to knock on your door—he would normally just come bouncing in. I took one look at him and knew it was bad. I stood up and instinctively reached out to embrace him. He stood with his head on my shoulder weeping over Edith's diagnosis: amyotrophic lateral sclerosis (ALS, or Lou Gehrig's disease). After a few moments his sense of feeling very alone in ministry within his denomination became apparent when he said to me, "They call only when they need a place to preach or need money." The "they" he was talking about were the officials from the denomination.

While this was going on I was thinking that I didn't want to be in this place in forty years. He had no one close. He had a lot of friends, but not a person or a peer he really trusted. In fairness, some of it was on him. He didn't participate in many ministerial events. He was a bit independent, mostly because he didn't like some of the "politics." I would go to district meetings and some guys would ask with raised eyebrows, "How's Paul?" I would say, "Why don't you ask *him*?" I don't know if anyone ever did. But as he cried on my shoulder, there was no doubt that he felt uncovered.

We were a larger, influential church. If a smaller church had done some of the things we did, they would have gotten called on the carpet. Although we were very generous with missions, Rev purposely did not direct it through the Assembly of God's official channels. We also gave mission funds to non-Assembly missions. We didn't use the Assembly name on our church—we were just "Christian Life Church." Yet when district officials would come to preach, he was honoring and generous, always generous to guest ministry. He had been a traveling evangelist and I know he wasn't always treated well. We had a lot of guest ministers in—David Duplessis, Pat Robertson, Ben Kinchlow, Jessie Winley, Ed Cole, Marilyn Hickey, Benny Hinn, Nora Lamb. These were not Assembly of God people, but we also had Assembly evangelists and speakers. I drove many of these ministers back and forth from the hotels and airport, always taking the opportunity to pepper them with questions. Rev was very open to the moving of the Holy Spirit, and yet he was very old school in other ways. He never flinched when I came into the church with my long hair, even though he was very conservative about outward things. Churches for miles around us benefited from our evangelistic anointing as hundreds would filter out to their own congregations.

But now here he was with a death sentence hanging over his wife and I was the one who was there. It really scared me; my heart broke for him. Again, I didn't want to be there in forty years. Earlier that year I had an encounter in that same office. I was reading Ephesians 2 and noticed the verses about being citizens of God's household and God building a habitation. I had a scary thought. I had been to two Bible colleges, had planted a church, had come from a good church, yet no one had ever defined the church for me. I knew the doctrine of the church, the history, the programs, the structure, but there was never a class, a book, or a lecture on the church itself. Here I was, seeing this Ephesians 2 passage come to life as I studied the truth of what the church is. I was wondering if this would fit in the Assemblies wineskin.

Now, with Rev crying on my shoulder, I wondered what was next. I had been doing well those days. Penny and I had bought a house and I was doing a lot of the preaching, which was very unusual for this type of church, which truly embraced us. The leadership supported us. There was talk that I would be the next pastor. Rev was getting up in age and had a few medical challenges as well, but I was content—growing and learning. I loved the church and loved my pastor. Why did it seem that God was troubling the waters by putting a vision in me that may not fit?

8

If God Gives You a Word, You're Going to Need It

This was my world. It was a world away from the projects that I had grown up in. I had really been born again in every sense of the word. My high school principal came to hear me preach one day and just wept. He talked to Rev about me. It turns out that he was a believer and was faithful at the Presbyterian church in Turtle Creek. He opened doors for me to hold a Bible study there on a regular basis. If life had ended right there, I would have been totally satisfied and grateful. I had a beautiful wife I was crazy about. Both of us had come from broken homes. This made learning to be married hard because it was something we had not been taught a lot about or really seen modeled. The overriding philosophy of ministry among churches like ours was "Pray and read—that's all you need." Things like marriage ministry were not on our radar. Our premarital preparation was a half-hour meeting. After that, we were on our own to try to figure it out. The fact that we survived is a testimony of God's care and proof that when you put God first and love each other—no matter what, you can make it.

We wanted children and were not consistent in our use of contraceptive measures. But Penny wasn't pregnant as we approached the end of our fourth year of marriage. Actually I wanted children but was honestly afraid of the responsibility. I certainly didn't want them to have a repeat of my life and was particularly concerned about providing for them. You have to understand the context of our lives to grasp what happened next—and why God would do something that would make most believers raise their eyebrows. Please understand it's happened exactly one time in my life. The context in one word was we were *settled*—house, ministry, job, friends. Not long after Edith's diagnosis, I undertook a deep exploration of not just what the church *did* but also what it *was*. I was getting concerned about this "new wine" fitting into the wine skin that I loved, adored, and in all honesty, had an emotional attachment to. This was a conflict I had kept entirely to myself.

One Sunday night I preached on the Ephesians 4 gifts—of apostles, prophets, evangelists, pastors, and teachers. My emphasis was on the equipping part of believers. I had never heard anyone preach this, but I saw it clearly. There really wasn't any pushback from our church. Rev didn't bat an eye. Remember: we had been exposed to a lot of ministry. Our Pentecostal doctrine said we believed in apostles and prophets—we just never dared call anyone that. Our credential form we signed each year asked us if we were a "pastor," "evangelist," or "other." I always wondered what would happen if someone checked "other." That night Penny quizzed me about my message. "Are you sure about what you taught?" she asked. I think she perceived the conflict this could create. What happened next is, as I said, unusual. I was driving home from the office in my 1976 powder-blue Pinto and was on Harrison City Road as I shifted into third gear—when God spoke audibly to me: "I want you to start a New Testament church." After regaining control of the car I was in a state of confusion. I didn't even know what a New Testament church was. We didn't use that language. However, there was no doubt that I had heard God.

That day was our fourth wedding anniversary and I was trying to figure out how to drop this bomb on my wife! We had a big night planned, a drive into Pittsburgh to go to Mount Oliver to a famous restaurant. She looked great! On the way we talked about all kinds of things. Then at the restaurant after ordering our meal, I saw that Penny had a card for me. She always made the best cards with little drawings and rhymes. She slid it across the table and said, "I have something to tell you." I replied, "No, I have something to tell you!" That was not my plan, though—I had decided this would wait until tomorrow. I was never the most sensitive guy, but telling your wife on your anniversary that you're about to blow your life up didn't seem like a good idea. But now all of a sudden I realized I had to speak. I don't know how I said it or what words came out of my mouth. But when I told her, she simply looked across the table at me and said, "Okay." She didn't ask me any more questions. She didn't tell me I had lost my mind—nothing. She just said, "Okay—great."

Then Penny said, "Open your card." When I opened the envelope I took out a card with a note from her doctor that read, "Congratulations, Mrs. Tucci! You're pregnant!" with a little drawing of a baby holding a banner that said, "Hi, Daddy!" I got up from the table and ran outside the restaurant and screamed. I was so excited that I could not contain myself. This was quite a day! Now some of this made sense. Why had God spoken to me in such an undeniable way? To this day I believe that if I had known Penny was pregnant, I wouldn't have been able to launch out and leave the security I had. I just don't think I would be able to do it.

Please remember: the church was in a sensitive place. Edith was sick and my news to them was not going to go over well. It took a lot of courage for me to talk to Rev and the board. They were understandably stunned, and very few comments were made. It was quite a meeting. Before the meeting I agonized over the decision, even though I had had an audible word to fall back on. In my spirit I heard the Lord again: "If you love this church, you will leave it." And I *did* love it—maybe a bit too much. I still do. Just recently, thirty-five years later, they went through a pastoral change, and I was invited to speak for them several times. The Holy Spirit moved.

God is good and He loves His Church. There's a great lesson to learn here. Simply put, if God gives you a word or a confirmation, you're going to need it. He's not trying to thrill you—He's trying to *move* you. That spiritual manifestation is not a credential—it's a warning. It's for spiritual warfare— to empower proper decision making. I've seen many believers receive supernatural confirmations and still miss it because they did not understand why God had given them the word.

I remember speaking one time at a large church in California when a man and his wife came forward for prayer. As I went to pray for them, I had a very clear word of knowledge. I told them that I saw them signing papers and that they were excited about it, but God was not in it—it was a trap. They literally turned white and said that they had just come from the real estate office where they had agonized over the purchase of a new home, which was going to be a stretch for them. Now you would think that when someone gets a word like that, it would be an easy decision. But the truth is that when God gives you a word like that, it's because it will *not* be an easy decision. I didn't know these people; I had never met them and didn't know their names. But the Holy Spirit was faithful to them.

My relationship with Rev became a little strained after my announcement. He was never unkind to me and never brought up the terrible timing of my decision in light of Edith's condition. To this day I believe God had to get me out of there or things would have just been put into my lap. I probably would have created a mess. Several officials from the Assemblies came to meet with me. They were kind, sincere men who knew me a little. The prevailing opinion seemed to be that I had lost my mind. I was the fair-haired kid in our district who was close to inheriting a very influential church at an unprecedented age. They were also concerned that I would draw members away by my leaving. I assured them that was not the case. Besides, we were far enough away and on the wrong side of town to have much appeal. They were concerned as they knew Rev was not on top of his game, especially with Edith's situation. I felt bad and I could not argue with these folks who thought I was somewhat of an idiot. At least these godly men didn't actually call me that. When I shared with them about wanting to have relationships and never be in Rev's situation, one of the men, Ron, seemed very empathetic. I think he saw himself in a similar situation and he told me, "I wish you well."

About a year later, Edith died. I kept in contact with everyone but of course it was different. Rev retired to Florida. I would call him and we would talk. I still remember one conversation we had about the quality of conversions. He was troubled by how much maintenance churches like mine did to assure folks stayed in the fold—programs we did that Christian Life had never done. His insights into it, I thought, needed to be heard. You can't get people saved who aren't lost! His question was "Are people really being converted?" Penny and I went to visit him in Florida and he lived only a few more years. That was the last time we saw him. I still miss him with his silver hair and red face—"Mister!"

Looking back to the time when Rev retired, I met with the church board without his knowledge. I still had a good relationship with them— they were good men but had little instruction on how to take care of a pastor, as evidenced by his also being the janitor for a time. Rev lived in the parsonage—a home owned by the church. It was purchased years before when he had first come to town. It was run down, but over the years with help from guys in the church, it was transformed into a nice house. They were seeing that new pastoral candidates had no desire to live in a parsonage. Why have something that was counted toward your salary that you could not take with you? It was worse than renting. So I proposed that they give him the proceeds from the sale of the house, which would have been a handsome amount. He had served well. He had led the church in tremendous growth and had a great reputation. He had presided over two major building campaigns and was certainly never overpaid. Some of the men could not comprehend what I was saying. They were not hostile, but they were just not understanding the principle of honor and blessing. Others were more open.

They agreed to give him a $25,000 blessing. It could have and should have been more, but in those circles this was a new standard. To help you understand their thinking, at one point they had decided to purchase a car for Pastor Ridings. This would be, of course, part of his salary. Rather than let him pick his own car or give him a budget, they sent a tight-fisted guy and he came back with the most stripped-down version of a vehicle you could purchase. The only option was an automatic transmission. Today you couldn't even buy a car like this. Several years later when it was time to replace the car, I spoke up. I insisted that they give me a budgeted amount and let me pick the car. Then I pushed the envelope a bit. I went to the Oldsmobile dealer, and though it took me several days, I got a great deal. The dealer was interested in having the pastor of a reputable church driving one of his cars. It was a new Oldsmobile Cutlass—gold with wire wheels and all the options such as air conditioning and power windows.

Rev told me it was the nicest car he had ever owned. His oldest son asked me to speak at the funeral, but several of Rev's kids were still somewhat awkward toward me, not realizing everything that had gone on behind the scenes. I was never quite able to explain everything to them. So as a result they bypassed me in regard to speaking at the funeral. I was disappointed but not angry. I was grieving, having suffered a real loss.

Years later when Lee called me about our father dying, it was totally different. I went home that night and Penny said, "Anything you want to tell me? Anything interesting happen today?" She actually knew about his death. I said, "No"—it had literally escaped my mind. The next day I was working out in the yard and was in a foul mood. Penny finally asked what the problem was and I realized I was so angry because I had no sense of loss at my father's death. To this day when families go through times of bereavement, I tell them what a gift it is to have a sense of loss and how privileged they are to love and be loved by somebody.

9

Building on a New Foundation

How to plant a church—*not!* It was our second church plant. Penny and I had no place to meet with the new church, no money, and in all honesty this church plant was a very difficult vision to sell, since I hardly knew what I was doing or what this New Testament church thing was. We didn't have a plant team or a core—all the things I would insist upon today if someone were planting a church.

The first week we met in the VFW hall in East Pittsburgh; about one hundred people showed up—most of them well-wishers who came just to encourage us, and I was grateful for that. The next day I got a phone call from the VFW board and was told we were no longer welcome to meet there because they found out we spoke in tongues. This group of Italian leaders of the VFW were part of the local Catholic church that had been majorly impacted by the charismatic renewal, which was not to their liking. So in our second week I had to quickly scramble and did find another place to meet: a funeral home. It wasn't a nice funeral home; it was an old, ugly, broken-down funeral home in the worst part of town. In the room where I stood to speak there was a curtain behind me, and any reasonable person would have wondered if there was a body back there.

The next week, when we began meeting at the funeral home, we had eleven people; that number included two guys I had been discipling (the one brought his girlfriend and the other his wife) and Dan, the guy we got the "Blessing Mobile" from. One friend reached out to a young couple who were spiritually hungry. This was in 1982, and that couple is still part of the church today. How about that? As for the fellow who brought his wife, we sent him out to plant a church several years later. So our beginning didn't look too good, but I had a word from God—literally. We also had Leo and Debbie, who another pastor sent to us as our worship leader (Leo). We ended up becoming great friends and Leo was with us for about six years and then was part of a church plant. Eventually we met at the Holiday Inn, which was a much better place for services.

A group of college students from the University of Pittsburgh started trickling in. Some of them had been involved at Penn State University in the middle part of the state. There they were part of a ministry that sounded very similar to what God had put on my heart and were able to help me process these things. We were a small-group church, although I did not know one other church that did small groups. By the time our church had reached one hundred in attendance, we would actually have more people in attendance in small groups than in our Sunday morning services. Small groups were at the core of what we were doing; it accomplished raising up leaders, getting people connected to one another, as well as creating groups doing acts of service and evangelistic outreach. Our small groups also went to the "abortuaries" (abortion centers), helped to pastor the church, and oversaw numerous ministries.

In our third year we opened up the discipleship training center, which we affectionately called the "whole-way house" instead of "halfway house." This was for ex-offenders who needed a new life and a new start. Several years before this we had met Gail Diana. Her in-laws brought her to church. She had two little boys who were very rowdy, and not long after that, she committed her life to Christ. Her husband, John, was in jail at the time for shooting a man in an armed robbery. John's parents were praying believers, and somehow to this day no one knows how John managed to get out of jail and escape a mandatory sentence. This just didn't happen when you have serious felonies you are found guilty of. Amazingly he eventually became the director of the "whole-way house"! Gail had visited him in jail and told him about her conversion, explaining that her life was different now. She made it very plain to him that if he were planning to come home, he had to go to church. That first Sunday she woke him up to go and he made it clear that he had no intention of fulfilling his promise. She told him, "Don't be here when I get home." He couldn't believe that she was serious!

The Holy Spirit showed up, ambushing John, and he was saved. I still remember him at the altar crying out to Jesus. I had preached a strong message that day on being a disciple and not just a believer. He cried out to Jesus, "I want to be a disciple! I want to be a disciple!" and indeed he became one. Who could have guessed at that moment that he would be the guy who would succeed me in just over seven years as pastor?

After his conversion John went to work with secular rehabilitation programs and was so frustrated with their lack of fruit that we went out on a limb with the help of a friend and businessman to open up a discipleship training center. This was "in the trenches" working with guys who had very rough lives and had been involved in criminal behavior and drug addictions.

We learned how to disciple, love, and share our lives with these men. This was also a great training opportunity for other men who felt they were called to ministry. I still strongly recommend jail ministry as a great training opportunity. It knocks the glamor out of ministry and helps you to understand how much work is really involved; it doesn't allow you to preach the gospel in the vacuum of your own life and experience.

John developed into a real student of the Word and a great teacher, and it was obvious that he had a pastor's heart and mantle on his life. I would show up at his house early every Saturday morning and he would make breakfast while we planned the day. The first stop was going into the Allegheny County jail, where we would preach to the prisoners and then follow up on guys who were out of jail. I have a saying in ministry that goes like this: "Ministry is spelled *follow up*, or you may say *follow through*. Good ideas are in abundance but it's the ones who know how to follow up and follow through who get the fruit."

When our church was thrust into not only local but also national attention and there weren't enough hours in the day, John and Gail were like anchors. Few churches could have gone through what we were going through, let alone continue growing without people like this. Penny and I have never lost our appreciation for the top-quality people the Lord has put into our lives. Jesus told us to pray for workers, not spectators. We have always invited folks to join us in what we were doing, and to be honest, we asked a lot of them. We have also valued their support. We come from a perspective that ministry is a privilege and that people will serve if it's clear what they are accomplishing. Aside from the Word of God and the Holy Spirit, people are our greatest resource; strategy is critical, but people are precious. I continue being amazed by how He sends us not just great helpers but covenant relationships as well.

Our wedding day with the Rev.

Training the next generation to pray at the altar.

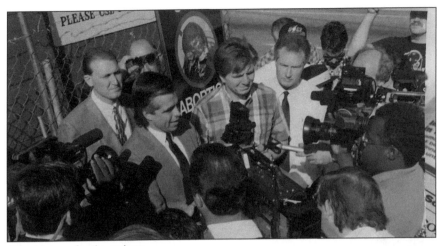

Speaking up for the unborn.

Washington Times

SUNDAY, SEPTEMBER 11, 1994 | PAGE A9

Congressman, ambassador help win release of pro-lifers

By John Waller
SPECIAL TO THE WASHINGTON TIMES

CAIRO—Three pro-life writers were released from custody yesterday after the intervention of a congressman and an ambassador, and one of those held demanded to know why a State Department security man set the detention process in motion.

The Rev. Keith Tucci of Melbourne, Fla., told reporters his ordeal began when Undersecretary of State Tim Wirth and a female pro-choice activist spotted him Friday at a press briefing at the U.N. population conference in Cairo.

A member of Mr. Wirth's security detail challenged Mr. Tucci's press credentials and arranged for U.N. security to have him detained for a security check, witnesses said. Mr. Wirth heads the U.S. delegation at the conference.

Mr. Tucci and two journalists who accompanied him, Sharon Turner of True Majority and David Haddon of the SCP Journal, spent the night at an airport hotel expecting to be deported. Egyptian police and U.S. security personnel were present.

The three, whose press credentials were confiscated Friday, were released after U.S. Ambassador Ned Walker spoke with Egyptian Foreign Minister Amr Moussa. Their credentials were restored.

U.S. Embassy officials declined to comment on the case.

Rep. Christopher H. Smith, New Jersey Republican, quoted U.S. and Egyptian security officials as saying a U.S. nongovernmental organization had named Mr. Tucci in connection with acts of violence at abortion clinics in Florida.

Mr. Tucci was a director of Operation Rescue International. Operation Rescue is a pro-life group that has blocked access to abortion clinics in the United States. Its members have courted arrest to press their views.

An FBI check showed that no warrant was outstanding for Mr. Tucci, Mr. Smith told reporters.

"Mr. Wirth's right-hand man said Mr. Wirth ordered him to check my credentials. I don't think he lied. I would like to ask Mr. Wirth what instigated him to ask that question," said Mr. Tucci, who was given press credentials as a correspondent for the Cabarrus County News of North Carolina.

Mr. Smith identified the security man as John Burton, a special agent in the diplomatic security service.

Mr. Wirth "should know that you don't haul people off when somebody calls you a bad name. People should not have to be subjected to that kind of political scrutiny ... to these Gestapo-type methods to silence people," Mr. Smith said.

"How can we be looking for jus-

tice when somebody who's an outspoken opponent of the people that happen to be in power can be carted off in broad daylight with no apology?" he said.

Mr. Tucci said the female activist is with the Feminist Majority Foundation, but he could not identify her further. Members of the group denied they had mentioned Mr. Tucci to the U.S. delegation.

Mr. Tucci denied that he or his current group, Life Coalition International, had broken the law.

● *This article is based in part on wire service reports.*

Egyptian arrest article.

Dave Williams/*The Wichita Eagle*

Wichita police arrest the Rev. Keith Tucci of Operation Rescue on an outstanding misdemeanor warrant Monday, before a public meeting began featuring Attorney General Janet Reno.

Tucci finds law waiting at airport

By Stephanie Reitz
FLORIDA TODAY

While his friends were demonstrating Saturday, Keith Tucci was flying in a Delta jet toward an arrest that he correctly guessed was imminent upon his arrival in Melbourne.

An arrest warrant on contempt of court

TUCCI

charges had been issued Monday after the Operation Rescue National executive director failed to appear to testify in the trial of pro-life activists charged with violating a court-ordered buffer zone around a Melbourne clinic that performs abortions.

Tucci was arrested Wednesday night in Pennsylvania, then released the next day after saying he would surrender following the group's Cities of Refuge campaign that ends today.

Boarding the plane in Atlanta, Tucci joked with a reporter to have a notepad handy and not be surprised if officers surrounded him when the plane landed at Melbourne International Airport.

At 5:05 p.m., three Melbourne police met Tucci at the jet and escorted him across the runway, away from startled passengers.

"Well, you guys didn't disappoint me," Tucci said.

"We wouldn't do that," police Capt. Gary Allgeyer answered as an officer guided Tucci away. He had one request — that he be allowed to take his Bible out of his carry-on luggage.

He is being held without bail at the Brevard County Detention Center.

NOVEMBER, NOVEMBER 19, 1993

National pro-lifer talks at FWB rally

By JEFF NEWELL
Daily News Staff Writer

Pro-life activists were urged to travel to Pensacola early this morning to protest at an abortion clinic, but not to risk arrest, an Operation Rescue official said during a rally Thursday night.

Johnny Hunter, a pastor and leader of Operation Rescue in Buffalo, N.Y., made the announcement shortly after Keith Tucci, national Operation Rescue executive director, finished an evening of music, preaching and praying before about 150 people at the Fort Walton Beach Municipal Auditorium.

The announcement followed several days of speculation that Tucci's appearance would signal the launch of a series of actions in Pensacola aimed at closing abortion clinics there.

But that was unclear Thursday.

Tucci, also pastor of the non-denominational Family Life Church in Melbourne, said he would not be with the group expected to gather near the Municipal Auditorium, at 7:15 this morning, before it proceeds to Pensacola.

KEITH TUCCI
... Operation Rescue director

Melbourne. But Tucci said he expects to return to Northwest Florida in early January.

Tucci was at the center of a simmering summer of clinic closures in Wichita, Kan., where 2,600 abortion foes were arrested for blocking clinics over a seven-week period. Most recently, he made headlines after being arrested for contempt of court in Philadelphia on a Florida warrant and held on $200,000 bond. He was released and arrested again for refusing to testify against anti-abortion demonstrators when he arrived in Melbourne.

He also organized a boot camp in Melbourne for those demonstrating at abortion clinics, schooling them in tactics, gathering information and infiltrating clinics.

Navarre resident Randy Hinesley, an organizer for Parents Against Child Killing, said the Pensacola clinic targeted today is The Ladies Center.

"But we won't be blocking the doors," said Hinesley, who recently pleaded no contest and was placed on probation for a charge of

Please see RALLY/6A

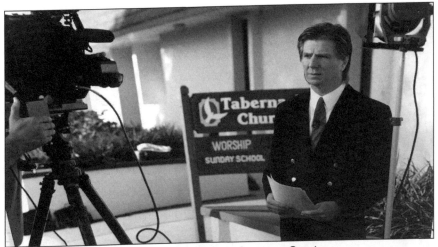

Press conference regarding case we won in Supreme Court.

Press conference with international reports after release from Cairo jail.

Gary Paladin, John Diana, and I. Gary would later be sent out to plant a church.

Defending the unborn in Robbinsdale, Minnesota with our good friends, Brian and Jacque Lother.

Gates of death camp in Washington D.C.

Metro News article. Tucci speaks up.

The man who caused a stir at the
United Nations Conference.

Setting in as NRP overseer, with incredible leadership team.

Penny & I enjoyed one of our children's weddings.

The Tucci Tribe

CHAPTER
10

How God Moves You

I believed the Lord wanted us to plant a church, but not close by. I had my eyes on Charlotte, North Carolina. This was a more normal church-planting strategy, targeting a growing area rather than a depressed area on the rough side of town. We put a lot of work into it. I interviewed a lot of pastors from that area, found out which side of town was growing, made several trips, and began choosing a church plant team. A couple who had attended our church in Pittsburgh had moved to Charlotte for their careers and were very excited about being part of the plant. I had a couple picked out who I thought would really work well as the pastoral team. Our leaders were excited about doing it. We had a businessman step up who wanted to make a big investment to make it happen.

Then something funny happened—instead of sending somebody, I came to believe that we were the ones who were supposed to go. Just recently I was talking to a good friend, Pastor Steve Crombie, of the River Church in Fairbaux, Minnesota. He was sharing with me that he was certain that he was called to go to South America. As a result of that, he altered his lifestyle, made career choices, and then when the pastoral role in his local church opened up because of a crisis, he was more prepared than he could have ever been otherwise. I think if you talk to a lot of men and women whom you see being used by God, many of them could identify with his and my stories. We need to learn how to "get our sails up" and let the Holy Spirit move us in the direction He chooses to. Jesus said in John 3:8 that those who are born of the Spirit are like the wind. We see the effects of the wind but can't determine its course; we see its effect but can't generate it. What we can do is have our ship in order, our mast secured, and our sails repaired from past storms so that He can drive our ship.

Pastor Mike Frie of Metro Harvest Church near Milwaukee tells the same kind of story. He felt called to go to Israel as a young man. He put his life in order and did it, living and serving there at poverty level yet excited and full of joy. All of a sudden he was interrupted with an urgent sense that he had to go home. He wasn't even close to having the funds to do it and was wrestling with leaving. He told no one and several days later woke up and found a bunch of money in his suitcase. He asked the other young guys he was living with if they knew anything about it. One came forward and told him he was impressed to give him the funds he had been relying on. Mike was obedient to go home and, through a series of events, married and became a pastor.

It's one of those "heaven questions" that we will someday perhaps ask: "How was I so sure about something and it ended up not coming to fruition?" We never did plant the church in Charlotte, but the preparation we did enabled us to do something we would not otherwise have planned for, which was my leaving our church, Word and Worship Fellowship, as the senior pastor. I do have some divine suspicions about some of these things; I think sometimes God works to get our bags packed and we think we're headed somewhere—but He's actually laying something out there to get our attention.

The first week we held church at the VFW, one of the families who came was the family of a young lady we had helped who had gotten pregnant out of wedlock. She had been one of the youth leaders where I was associate pastor at the time. I remember telling her, "You can't get married because the guy is a jerk, and you can't have an abortion." Driving home that day, I pondered the question of why she couldn't have an abortion. I knew it was clear that she shouldn't, but honestly I could not have given you one scripture to back it up.

Penny had been doing some research at the Christian television station where she worked regarding the positions of the two candidates for president at the time—Jimmy Carter and Ronald Reagan. She was preparing a paper to help people decide who to vote for. During that process, one of the major political platform issues she studied was that of abortion—who was for it and who was against it. Although Carter had strongly promoted his Christianity, he had voted for abortion consistently, while Reagan held the opposite position. Penny did some thorough investigation about abortion and what all it entailed. Nightly she would come home and talk it over with me, because she was deeply disturbed about what abortion actually was. We, along with much of the church, had been uninformed and ignorant of this before that point. She had even looked into the methodology of abortion and how cruel and unthinkable it was. The humanity of the child, its little fingers, its heartbeat, all forty-six chromosomes at the moment of conception—all that we would ever be, male or female, redheaded or left handed, athletic or artsy—each fearfully and wonderfully made, was present at conception. Abortion was now not just an "issue"; it was little boys and girls who were being brutally killed and needed a voice—it was personal. What Penny had studied and consequently shared helped to put a foundation in my heart and mind about the travesty of abortion, which ultimately directed a critical part of the ministry God had called me to.

I had become very close with this young lady's family. Her father had previously had a hard heart toward God and was on the outskirts of the church, but through his daughter's crisis pregnancy we became friends. His daughter's pregnancy caused him to do a great deal of self-evaluation and call out to God. They also happened to live very close to where we were planting this new church, unlike many other people we knew at the time. When they came that first week, they were very clear to tell me that they were just there to support us and thank us for all that we had done for their family and to wish us the best. A couple of weeks later they showed up at church again. The vision I had laid out that first week was something that kept coming back to them. Roy was the father; he and Maxine would become major players in Word and Worship Fellowship for years to come.

At one point Roy lost a good job with the railroad when they were cutting back their services. He then worked several jobs as a mechanic, and he was a very good one. A group of guys from our church got together and helped to fund Roy in a start-up business that was built around front-end alignments. God tremendously blessed the business and I think Roy and Maxine probably brought more people into the church during our time there than any other people. In all my years in pastoral ministry, they are the only people I ever told that they were giving too much money. Instead, I encouraged Roy to reinvest some of that money back into his business, and he did—then he gave even more money! Royanne was his daughter—the one we had helped with her pregnancy. Roy and Maxine were members of the church for over thirty years until they each passed away. It was a deep honor to officiate both of their home-goings to heaven after thirty-plus years of faithful service.

Roy had played a really important role in my life as an encourager. He was never a guy who was going to be out front and preaching, but he would whisper things in my ear that would later be significant.

Maxine opened her home and we literally overran it for several years because of her hospitality and her geographical proximity. Royanne later married and she and Pete remain pillars in Word and Worship Church today (the name of the church was changed to Bridge City Church in 2019). Their second son, Austin, was on staff at the church for several years. Royanne's dilemma would be something God used to chart my destiny. Through her and Penny, God had helped to awaken my heart to the cries to the unborn and their mothers. Having studied this after my initial confrontation with the issue, I could now give you book and verse on the sanctity of life.

We also had post-abortive young ladies coming into the church and their pain pierced my heart. We began to be active. Our church started an organization called the Association of Christian Churches. We hired a dear lady named Val, who was a "Holy Spirit case worker"—counseling girls, training workers, and helping equip other local churches. We also started going to the killing places (abortion centers) to pray and offer alternatives. The more we did, the more opportunities came, usually dressed up as challenges. There were legitimate needs for medical care for moms who were choosing life. There were women whose boyfriends had thrown them out. There were families who had financial needs. There were those that needed follow-up and counseling. There were churches asking questions. The media was magnifying everything we were doing. Meetings with volunteers took loads of time and energy. Already we were running into legal problems, so developing relationships with the legal community was important. The media, for the most part, did anything they could to discourage those who were supporting us.

Then on Mother's Day 1987, God had a surprise for me. In those days Pittsburgh had a Democratic Party mayor who was very pro-life, Richard Caligiuri, who would lead the Mother's Day march. There were speakers and festivities. With a good core of faithful, pro-life activists, the group had managed to secure a speaker to talk about Operation Rescue. At that time no one had heard of it. So here were all these politicians on the platform and this guy started talking about blocking the doors of "abortuaries." You had to be there to fully appreciate the irony of it.

For the previous couple of years our church had been leading teams into the Soviet Union. I had been arrested twice there. People were coming from all over the United States to be trained by our team to make covert trips. In 1979 I was standing in front of a huge world map on which was a line highlighting major Christian crusades and evangelistic thrusts—along with a stark line referred to as "the iron curtain" with nothing behind it. As I stood there looking at it, I heard the Lord in my spirit say, "I'm going to send you there." I had no idea how that was going to happen and I can't say that I tried to make any plans to go. I would not have had a clue about how to go, but it did resonate in my spirit to give it prayerful attention.

At one of our Sunday gatherings at the Holiday Inn a new couple who had seen our sign out on the highway attended; a friend of theirs knew something of the church and had encouraged them to come. Aaron was a Chinese man who was raised in Taiwan because his family had escaped the Cultural Revolution in China. He had met his American wife, Jan, there, who was the daughter of an American soldier. Aaron was a nuclear engineer for the Westinghouse Corporation, which was headquartered not far from us. Because of his background, he had a natural heart for restricted-access nations and Jan was burdened for the world.

Aaron and Jan started attending regularly and told me about their desire to travel into the Soviet Union. I held my peace for a while because I really wanted to check them out. When I told Aaron that this was something in my heart, he began sharing many ideas. We met at his house every Friday for a year and prayed that God would lead us in regard to this mutual desire to penetrate the Iron Curtain. Westinghouse had sent Aaron to several of the Scandinavian countries for work. While he was there, he had made contact with church leaders in Finland and Sweden who were slipping in and out of the Soviet Union across the Baltic Sea (which was the easiest access point not to be detected while bringing in contraband materials). So we reached out to those friends, made a trip to Sweden, and got trained in how to handle ourselves. What to do and not to do was a more intense study than I would have imagined. We made our first trip and, by God's grace, connected with the believers the Swedish missionaries had orchestrated for us to meet.

One of my memories as we were boarding the boat to go across the Baltic Sea was looking up at the smokestack and seeing a very large hammer and sickle on it. That sent shivers down my spine. I grabbed Aaron and said, "Aaron, this is a Russian boat." "That's because we're going to Russia!" he replied. All this seemed like a great idea, a really cool strategy, a fun and exciting missionary activity, until that moment! But I was about to find out just how serious it really was.

Who would know that the Soviet Union was about to blow open and that within a few years we would not only have access but also huge crowds who would gather as we spoke? The pastors and churches we had secretly gone to support would now be pushed out front to be great spokesmen for God.

I was in Riga, Latvia, the night Soviet tanks rolled in to try to stem the tide of the cry for freedom from Soviet authority. The Latvians had torn down statues of Lenin and had replaced signs written in Russian with signs written in Latvian. Large blocks of limestone and sandbags were stacked in front of government buildings. It was a historic moment to be there to see this unfold. At one point I attempted to climb up on some of the barricades to preach to the crowd, but I was quickly discouraged by the rifle barrel that was put in my back, telling me clearly to stand down. Just several years later, Larry and Debbie Stout would be living in the Latvian embassy, recognized as the first legal missionaries since the fall of the Iron Curtain. Larry was one of the people who had been trained by us. He and Debbie and their family had seventeen years of faithful service there and made a huge impact.

Aaron ended up going full time as a missionary, leaving his job with Westinghouse and traveling the world helping to plant churches and training Chinese nationals. Once again God had sent us an incredible person who was ready to be used. Aaron and Jan had just recently been filled with the Holy

Spirit and were looking for a spiritual church that would embrace them. It still amazes me to this day as I look back during that time frame when I think of the incredible nucleus God put together. Maybe that had something to do with the urgency with which we were called out of Christian Life Church.

But now here I was on the streets of Pittsburgh listening to a man talk about "higher laws." I understood—I had been arrested in the Soviet Union for violating their laws. I had a very clear theology in this matter and had given it much thought. I had studied the doctrine of lesser magistrates and had biblical clarity in regard to state authority and biblical allegiance. The idea the speaker presented was something I had never considered from a tactical standpoint, but his argument of employing higher laws was certainly scriptural. My life was about to change again!

CHAPTER

—————— 11 ——————

You Can't Pray in Your House

E ven before I got arrested in the USSR, as well as arrested in front of "abortuaries" (I hate referring to places that kill children as "clinics"—clinics heal people), I had the occasion to understand that believers at times must gracefully resist unjust laws, jurisdictions, or applications. We lived in Penn Hills in a nice middle-class neighborhood. We had moved specifically to be closer to the church, but we were still in a different municipality. Each week we held a small group meeting at our home with usually about fifteen people in attendance. Some would linger until about 9:30 p.m. and we had parking in our driveway, so only three or four additional cars were ever on the street. We usually had a time of worship led with an acoustic guitar. We had never had a complaint from a neighbor.

I was served a notice of a code violation for operating a church out of my home. I was sure there was some confusion. I personally went and met with the city manager, being sure some mistake was made. He told me in no uncertain terms that this was not the case, that the town was pursuing this matter and was going to shut us down! I turned the documents over to a very competent lawyer in our church who later became a judge. She assured me that it was a mistake—that the code had to do with building violations and such. Soon she found out what I had also come to discover—someone was grinding an axe.

At the hearing she completely debunked the complaint; the town was obviously not prepared for her. The judge, however, said he would mail us the decision. Usually when the matter of self-incrimination comes up, you think of the witness, not the judge. The judge found me guilty, but the decision he wrote was so over the top that it led me to believe that if you prayed over your meal at dinner, you could be guilty of running a church in your house.

I sent the decision to the local newspaper with a comment that we would continue meeting, and the newspaper published the judge's decision. I happened to be away the day it came out and got a call from Penny saying, "You need to come home." "Why?" I asked. She said, "For starters, the mayor is in the living room, the town's phone lines are being overwhelmed, and city council members are having neighbors at their doors." We did absolutely nothing inconsiderate to provoke the charges and we did nothing to provoke the response except to use the judge's own words. It all went away and the judge blamed the city, while the mayor blamed the city manager. We came out looking good and handled ourselves well. I had no idea that this little incident was preparing not only me but also our church for what was around the corner.

We never did get to the bottom of the whole thing—it was demonic, the proverbial tempest in a teacup—but it opened my eyes to the fact that just because you are doing righteous things doesn't mean the world will celebrate you. It also made me aware that in a crisis a leader does not have the luxury of being fearful; people are watching you—people who need courage for their own lives. Sometimes a leader can get tunnel vision about what he or she is up against and miss the opportunity to impart courage to those who are watching.

Speaking of the demonic, it's a subject that is sensationalized on one hand and ignored on the other hand. Jesus gave us the authority to cast out devils. In any type of warfare, if you refuse to identify your enemy, your ability to defeat him or her is all but lost. Jesus told us to love our enemies, not to pretend that we don't have any or only to do or not to do things that would cause us to have enemies. Much of antiseptic Christianity is built around a false theology of thinking that if enemies rise up against us, then somehow we must not be like Jesus. We need to remember Peter's sermon at Pentecost, when he quoted Psalm 110:1: "Sit thou at my right hand, until I make thine enemies thy footstool." So God has enemies and if we are in covenant with Him, shouldn't His enemies be our enemies as well? It takes clear vision to see who or what is standing in the way and to identify the obstruction without apology. The United States was losing the battle against terrorism until our leaders were willing to identify it as Islamic in nature.

My brother Lee was into Ouija boards when he was a kid; that was all I ever knew about spirits. One night after a "kook group" meeting soon after my conversion, I was driving away from the meeting location when I suddenly became aware that there was a being—a thing—in the front seat. I could see it out of my peripheral vision, and I was as scared as I ever had ever been in my life. Those ladies in that group did not talk about the devil a lot and I had never heard of anything like this. A guttural voice said, "Look at me," several times. I drove on and kept my eyes forward, but its silhouette was still discernible in my side vision. Thankfully this lasted for only a few minutes. I never looked, and I said nothing. Ironically, after that I was not afraid, but I knew there was a devil as stated in the Bible, and like other things in the Bible that I had come to know were true, so was he.

Not long afterward at one of the "kook group" meetings, a young lady in her 20s who was as sweet and nice as could be—nothing like the background that I had come from—was in the meeting. About halfway through, a demonic manifestation came through her, illustrating the fact that people who do not believe in the devil are able to do so because his plan is to be ignored rather than cast out.

After I had spent several months in Bible school, a motorcycle guy began attending our Sunday night services. He was out of place in this middle-class congregation but was welcomed and embraced. He had a horrific scar that covered a large part of half of his face. If memory serves me right, he had told those who were ministering to him conflicting versions of what had happened to him. He was very needy and a group of students with good intentions tried working with him, but they were in over their heads.

One Sunday night he walked in and went to sit down beside some of these students. All of a sudden as I was sitting behind them, I could see into the spirit realm; it was much like viewing an X-ray inside his body, and I saw a ghoulish-looking creature. The guy sat down in the pew and put his head on the shoulder of one of the young guys there, trying to befriend him. This thing that I saw attached to the fellow had long fangs that it stuck into the guy as he sat down next to him. I had never heard of or seen anything like this. My eyes were wide open—I was seeing the creature just as I was seeing the guy it was attached to. In a few minutes a couple of the young men led him out of the service into a back room. I wasn't exactly sure of what to do, but I couldn't believe God had shown me that and didn't want me to do anything.

I walked into the back lobby down the hallway and I could hear what room they were in. I'm not saying what I did about this is the right way to have tried consoling him, but I just yelled out, "Come out of him in the name of Jesus!" Of course, these guys had no idea of what was going on, but in a moment they would! He was not a small man, but he contorted himself and jumped up on the window ledge and began chanting, "There is no Trinity!" It's interesting—nobody had said anything about the Trinity. The students started yelling at me to leave as if I were the one who was denouncing the Trinity. They did not want to talk about it afterward, claiming that I was immature and over-zealous. To my knowledge, his behavior with them went on. Not long after that, he was shot and killed by a man whose wife he was bothering. Those are very dramatic manifestations; they certainly are not everyday occurrences. There was never a pattern of these things; indeed, I never had another experience like either of those.

Historically, the church seems to swing from completely ignoring the devil to almost being more conscious of him than the Lord Himself. What I have come to believe is very simply this: The enemy will almost always choose to go undetected and unrecognized. The old saying "I'd rather deal with a known devil than an unknown devil" really does have some merit. The demonic manifestations I have personally witnessed seem to fall into two different categories: (1) The enemy is discerned and pressured and then manifests himself in a desperate act of intimidation. (2) There is so much demonic control going on that the enemy flaunts his presence. This often happens because there is no one present who knows how to deal with him.

These encounters helped prepare me for the demonic activity that we would encounter in exposing the shedding of innocent blood. I've had numerous encounters over the years with people who would be considered well-educated, socialized folks in the abortion industry, and I've used my authority in Jesus's name to confront that evil. I don't share these things lightly, but we must be aware of the schemes of darkness, and we have no need to fear dealing with demons. The Scriptures are as clear on demonic activity as they are on God's goodness—neither can be ignored! There is a core of folks in the abortion industry who are offering blood sacrifices of aborted children; these are not sensational claims nor the claims of folks trying to instigate Christian abhorrence. As in Bible times, the offerings to Molech were the blood of innocent children. Psalm 106:37 (ESV) notes, "They sacrificed their sons and their daughters to the demons." I believe that some of these folks do this unawares; but there are more than you could count who know exactly what they're doing and it's their religion. That's why Proverbs 6:17 says that God hates the hands that shed innocent blood.

12

Chicken Sandwiches

After the Mother's Day march a group from Pittsburgh decided that they were going to go to New York City to participate in the first national "rescue" event, in which God-fearing Christians would passively and peacefully sit in front of the clinic doors to prohibit the killing of children. When I arrived at the abortion business, about four hundred believers had already made it there and were sitting down. The police had the street blocked off. Screaming pro-abortion supporters were cordoned off behind barricades. It reminded me of the prophets of Baal who were cutting themselves and screaming. I went into a nearby restaurant, sat down, and ordered a chicken sandwich. I would joke later that I did what most Christians do when something is happening—get something to eat.

I felt like everything was in slow motion. I just stared out the window. What was going on in my mind? I just came to watch this because I wanted to witness what was going to happen and how the doctrine of "higher laws" was going to be applied, but I already knew that my life was about to change and that God had brought me there to do more than eat a chicken sandwich.

We had encountered pro-abortion demonstrators before in Pittsburgh,

THE GOD OF INTERVENTIONS

but nothing like this. So I went over on their side and just mingled among them. Trust me when I tell you it was as if the mouth of hell were open. These weren't people with a political or philosophical agenda—this was not even about women's rights. This was about innocent blood and they wanted it spilled! For anyone who has never seen demonic activity or doubts that demons are real and manifest themselves in this present age, they should simply get involved and watch the desire that's being shrieked out to see children killed.

Eventually I made my way across the street and found myself sitting down. Just as a side note: the guy who sat down beside me was Mark Bravaro, all-star tight end of the New York Giants. By the end of the day we were all carted off to jail—and my life would never be the same! If you talk to pro-life people who have spent time in jail for righteous actions, almost unanimously they will tell you of the incredible fellowship and bonding that happens when you're incarcerated for the sake of righteousness. Most of us have experienced deep spiritual connections with people as we've worked on church projects, evangelism, or even foreign missions. But this *jail* connection really took things to another level. This is why many people who have been in jail together still remain connected.

Just a few years later, as we were preparing to plant a church in Charlotte (which never happened, as noted earlier), key core rescue leaders were meeting in D.C. I wasn't in attendance because of pastoral responsibilities. In every movement, leadership tensions and dynamics come into play. Operation Rescue had come to the place in which leadership needed to be more clearly defined. If you've ever been in a room full of passionate people, you can appreciate how tenaciously they cling to their opinions—especially those who are putting their lives on the line to back up those opinions. There were different philosophies, different denominational and doctrinal contexts, and certainly different personal allegiances. Somehow or other they settled on me as the compromise candidate to assume the leadership role for Operation

Rescue, an office I wasn't running for, by the way.

By this time Operation Rescue had become a lightning rod. Many people in our own congregation had been arrested for doing exactly what I had done in New York City. Rescues were happening all over the country and even in other countries. Many of the people doing rescues were pro-life but were more activist-oriented then gospel-oriented, so despite having the same desire and the same focus, we didn't always have the same orientation.

The way I found out that I was appointed as the new national director was as follows: Sally, our church secretary, came into my office and said, "There's a reporter on the telephone who wants your comment about being the new director of Operation Rescue." So while I had prepared the church for having John step into my role and Penny and me to take a team to Charlotte, we were at least prepared for a change. How was it that I was getting a call from a reporter before the group involved had even talked to me personally? I don't know. But it also explains some of the spontaneity and intensity in leading a movement.

Our leadership and church were totally supportive and prepared to send us out to assume the leadership of Operation Rescue. Of course, I had a lot of questions. I had an expanding role ministering at other churches, and our Soviet mission thrust was at full throttle. The iron curtain had fallen, and as my dear friend Dick Bashta said, "People were being saved by the acre." We had tremendous favor there because of my arrest prior to things opening up. Our church had just finished a building program and exciting, positive things were happening on a local level.

The pro-life movement up until that time had been manned primarily by committed Catholics; the evangelical and charismatic churches had been pretty much AWOL. God would use Operation Rescue to help make abortion a gospel, and not just a humanitarian, issue. I had the honor of working alongside many Catholics who loved Jesus and walked out their convictions. It's unfortunate that the Catholic church as a whole has not done the same thing in regard to standing for the unborn. It's my opinion that had the Catholic Church excommunicated pro-abortion politicians who claimed to be Catholics, the landscape would be different today. I do salute my Catholic brothers and sisters who were there while we were "eating chicken sandwiches."

Not long ago someone asked me how I had developed a national ministry. Maybe they were wondering, "How could *this* guy have a national ministry?" I had never really thought about that. I had never pastored a megachurch or had a media ministry. So I told them about my experience with Planned Parenthood. On a Saturday evening when I was still pastor of Word and Worship, a reporter called my home to ask if I had a comment on the lawsuit filed against me, our church, and over forty members. I didn't. I didn't even know we had been sued. This was no small endeavor—it was a federal, RICO lawsuit (racketeering, influencing, and corrupt organizations). The original law had been written to stop the mafia.

We would be the first church in American history to have a RICO lawsuit filed against us. Without realizing it, Planned Parenthood had put me on the national map. I was on television shows, radio shows, interviews with Christian and secular talk shows, and in newspaper stories. Maybe more significant than any other thing, this lawsuit gave me credibility with the committed core of pro-lifers who had been at it long before I showed up. This didn't last just for a week or month—it lasted for several years. It gave me a voice to other churches and Christian leaders such as Jerry Falwell and James Dobson. I was invited to address the national association of evangelicals. This didn't happen because I had a great idea or some special gift—it happened because Planned Parenthood had targeted me and God intervened. Then I got sued in different jurisdictions all across the country—almost anywhere I had spoken, been in a rally, or sat in front of the clinic. This was their new tactic, to try intimidating us. I ended up being on "Nightline," "Good Morning, America," "Firing Line with William F. Buckley" and many other programs and was arrested numerous times for non-violent passive intervention for the unborn.

13

So Now I'm Part of God's Mafia

Have you ever heard the phrase "Don't make a federal case about it"? I found out what it meant as I had lawsuits stacked up in my office in the corner behind the door. After our leadership met to figure out who was suing us and why, we realized that it was not just the local abortion operation but also involved national pro-abortion groups. This stratagem had connections to the brain trust of all the big national groups. They wanted to make an example out of us—but so did God!

To do this they had to admit that we were hurting their business, which in their mind was racketeering. They could not afford to allow the thought or news out that a small band of believers had caused this upheaval, so they painted us as thugs. Unfortunately, many courts would agree with them until we ultimately weaved our way to the Supreme Court over twenty years later! Of course, our church did not have the hundreds of thousands of dollars to defend such a lawsuit. I made contact with what are well-known legal groups today who were just getting started then. They were not able to help, but a few concerned lawyers reached out to their own firms in the Pittsburgh area. From them we received incredible legal help, even from a firm with RICO experience—and there was no charge! Some of them were pro-life, some were outraged at the misuse of the law, and some did it because other firms challenged them to pitch in. One firm joined in because they had a previous case with one of the firms who were suing us and they didn't like them. The enemy of my enemy is my friend!

Then an amazing thing happened—the head of the American Civil Liberties Union and a professor at a local Catholic college was asked by the media what he thought of the suit. He was not pro-life and the media was not expecting his answer. He said it was a violation of protected speech. I watched it on television and apparently so did some of our lawyers. He ended up using his legal class to do all the research, and his class handled many legal details as part of their training. The pro-abortion attorney's attempt to bury us in paperwork backfired. We more than matched them, and because there were over fifty defendants, that meant different lawyers on our team would be filing every conceivable document they could for their specific designated clients. That equaled a mountain of paperwork and lawyer's time, and we would learn later that the other side was not working for free.

This particular case never made it to trial. One of the abortion plaintiffs went out of business—we were told that they were unable to pay their legal bills. What a lot of folks don't understand today is that God used Operation Rescue to draw many legal minds into the fight for life. Jay Sekulow would certainly be one. I meet Jay in Atlanta during the Democratic National Convention, where we had gone to prophesy to the delegates about the shedding of innocent blood. His home was in Atlanta at that time and he came out to help us as he witnessed the mistreatment we were receiving from the police and the judicial system. At that time he was making a living running a conventional law practice, but not for long. His first national audience was on Barbara Walter's show regarding my case in Wichita, Kansas, where an out-of-control federal judge actually had me arrested while I was live on air at a Christian radio station. Mathew Staver, the founder of the Liberty Council, made his first Supreme Court appearance on my Florida case. We were arrested for walking down the sidewalk—not because of what we did but because of what we believed. We actually recorded a police officer saying, "That one has a Bible—arrest him!" This content-based discrimination was more common than you might believe.

14

They Can't Do That, Can They?

Although we managed to get the case dismissed in Pittsburgh, I was added to another RICO suit in Chicago, which we lost. Years later, that case would eventually be overturned by the Supreme Court. The pro-abortion strategy with RICO was intimidation—to go after our assets and our homes. If they could prove loss of income by "racketeering," we would lose everything. It was a good strategy—very intimidating. The Christian community owes a lot today to those pro-lifers who put themselves out there and risked everything. These unknown heroes are and will be celebrated in heaven.

Joe Scheidler of Chicago, who is considered the father of pro-life activism, particularly suffered under these attacks, but he fought back valiantly against the RICO attack. He and his wife put their home up as collateral for the Supreme Court appeal, where we emerged victorious, finally defeating the RICO hammer. We also owe so much to those early Christian lawyers, many of them fighting themselves to stay afloat, who gave untold hours and sacrificed their time and talent. Today the Christian legal community has more legal power than the ACLU. These organizations regularly prevail in their head-to-head battles.

The Alliance Defending Freedom, Jay Sekulow/ACLJ, the Liberty Council, the Thomas Moore Society, and others have won cases for me and many other pro-lifers. In addition to the legal victories, thousands of children were saved from the butcher's knife. And while we are in a downward trend in many areas of cultural influence, the Christian legal network is steadily gaining ground. Many of these men and women got started by coming to our aide—the battle draws warriors!

We once held a rally in front of a killing center in White Plains, New York. Several of my close friends, Pastor Joe Kelley and Mike Warren, spent time in jail for violating the judge's injunction. They didn't break any law; they were just there demonstrating faith. Again, we had an overbearing judge punishing folks for voicing their opposition to child killing.

Several years later I accepted a preaching engagement in the Catskill Mountains in New York. The pastor said, "When you get here there's somebody I want you to meet." After church a couple came up to me with a little girl, and the lady said, "We want you to meet our daughter. The day you were in front of the clinic in White Plains, I was inside, scheduled for an abortion. As you guys began to sing 'Amazing Grace,' I looked out the blinds. I remember specifically seeing you. I was convicted and changed my mind, and we just wanted to share with you that she's alive today and we're serving the Lord."

I have numerous stories like that one. Hundreds of freestanding abortion clinics—places whose only business was killing children—were put out of business just because pro-lifers took church to the doorsteps of hell. Through all of this I was arrested over fifty times. Over twenty-five of those times I was never charged with a crime! I never did anything wrong; they just wanted to silence the pro-life message. So I would spend a few hours or the night in jail and then no charges would be filed.

We had a saying we used sarcastically in the pro-life movement: "They can't do that, can they?" Because inevitably that's what uninitiated pro-lifers

THEY CAN'T DO THAT, CAN THEY?

would say when they saw things like that happening, like the gag orders we had in court that mandated that we could not mention the word abortion or the phrase *killing children*. Think of the words of the apostle Peter in 1 Peter 2:19 (ESV). "For this is thankworthy, if a man for conscience toward God endure grief, suffering wrongfully." This is part of Christian living, just like praying, tithing, and helping the needy. It's what happens when we follow Jesus—but the reality of "suffering wrongfully" seems to be lost in our present understanding of being a follower of Jesus. This doesn't mean that we will always be misjudged or accused or that we should look for trouble, but it certainly makes it clear that we should be willing to be made able by God's grace to be ill treated and not to fear walking out our love for God and the consequences that may accompany it.

I remember a Texas case in which I was representing myself; the abortionist was on the stand and I refused to call him by the title "Doctor." The prosecuting lawyer kept objecting, insisting that I call him "Doctor." The judge ordered me to do so as well. I told her, "I'll call him 'Doctor' if he can tell me what he cures. He snarled and said, "Pregnancy." I still didn't call him "Doctor" and they eventually gave up trying to make me do it.

There are some advantages when you represent yourself—you can get away with a lot more than a lawyer does. The judge in that case had ties to the abortion industry but would not recuse herself. The trial was over an injunction that was filed and that she granted to keep us away from the abortion clinic. An injunction is an order in which there essentially is no law, saying there is imminent harm or damage that's going to be done and it requires judicial intervention. When you violate an injunction you are found guilty of contempt of court. This is exactly what Daniel did when he refused to obey the king's order not to pray (see Daniel 6). When she brought me in from jail for my "show cause" hearing, she told me that if I would just apologize to the court—meaning her—she would let me go. I calmly told her she should apologize to God and to the citizens of Texas who elected her to uphold the law. It was a short hearing—she gave me six months!

We had simply been doing street preaching; we weren't on the abortion business property or doing anything illegal. We were next door to the clinic when the head of the National Organization for Women served the injunction on me from the judge. They later had a video of me tearing up the injunction and sprinkling it on her head. That's not exactly a good defense tactic, but I did enjoy the moment. Please remember that I still hadn't committed a crime. I've had Christian leaders tell me that they would not do anything that would result in them being falsely accused, so as to protect their ministry, and I'm not suggesting we should not take the stewardship of the sphere of ministry God has given us seriously. But Jesus was accused of things He did not do and things that He did that may have violated an unjust law but honored the law of God—and the servant is not above his master!

I remember making the collect call home to tell Penny that I was going to be in Texas for six months. Now anybody who knows her knows how much she had sacrificed and how supportive she had been through all of this. At this point we had five small children and I was often gone, speaking in churches and conferences. I was not just working on the pro-life front but was also deeply engaged in serving and encouraging pastors and their families. Many times she traveled with me, kids in tow, not always having the greatest accommodations.

On this occasion I knew the conversation was going to be more difficult. We had actually planned a vacation, something we weren't able to do much. Of course, my being in jail was going to ruin all that. But classically she took the news courageously and was willing to man the ship for however long was required. She wasn't overjoyed about it but was willing to do whatever was needed to stand with me in this cause.

We called Jay Sekulow and he came to see me within two days. I was out of jail in very short order—the Texas State Supreme Court overturned the judge unanimously! A young Christian lawyer sitting in the trial watching the kangaroo court was so convicted that he later ran against her and took her seat as judge. He took her sign off the door and mailed it to us.

I got to go home and we were able to go on our vacation. These injunctions became the favorite tactic of the abortion industry; they would tell the judge that we were going to do all types of awful things. Honestly if they could dream it up, they would say it. They even said one time that we had threatened to kidnap their children. Our lawyers would say, "There are already laws on the books to handle these alleged planned 'crimes,' so they can use those laws if they want to charge you with these things as opposed to using injunctions." Unfortunately, liberal judges often decided that pro-lifers weren't even allowed to stand and speak or sing, so we were in constant court battles over these injunctions.

A Florida judge issued an injunction and then demanded that I testify as to whether certain people were present when the injunction was violated; I refused to do that. He ordered me to stay in town, which I could not do, due to the fact that we had several pro-life meetings set up in other parts of the country. I had gone from San Jose to Minneapolis to Philadelphia. The word in San Jose and Minneapolis was that the police were trying to get me before I had left town, but that didn't work. I was arrested in Philadelphia and taken to the Philadelphia jail on $250,000 bond. The judge in Florida said that I had a twenty-one-year sentence awaiting me and that he was going to give me six months (which is the maximum for most injunctions). He was going to do it forty-two times for the forty-two people I wouldn't testify against.

When I went into the jail that night, it was overcrowded. There was no bunk space, but when the guys from the cell heard I had a $250,000 bond and that my name was Tucci, they thought I was part of the Philadelphia mob and instantly gave up their bunk. I told them that I certainly wasn't a mob member but was a preacher. They laughed and said, "Yeah, there are a lot of preachers in here!"

In the morning a local pro-life lawyer showed up with the sheriff and they took me out of the jail cell on what's called a writ of habeas corpus, which means to "present the body." Once again a righteous attorney understood that the arrest order the Florida judge had issued was invalid; he couldn't charge me with forty-two separate counts. As the sheriff and the lawyer were leading me out, the guys in the cell yelled, "Yeah, sure you're a preacher!" They obviously did not think a preacher would have the ability to be ushered out as quickly as I was.

When I flew back to Melbourne, Florida, I was arrested when I stepped off the plane and later sentenced to six months in jail. It was the beginning of December; there would apparently be no Christmas for our family that year. But Penny had a plan of making Christmas great for the kids—even if their dad was in jail. Amazingly, eighteen days later I got released on good behavior and made it home for Christmas. We had gone to visit Janet Reno when she was holding a town hall meeting in a large Baptist church in Wichita, Kansas. We wanted to ask her about a statement she had made against Christians. As we were sitting in the sanctuary, my friend next to me elbowed me and said, "Keith, they're coming to get you!" I hadn't done anything at all, yet I was arrested by the Secret Service and taken to the Wichita jail. The people taking me to jail were nice but refused to tell me why I had been arrested. They seemed embarrassed. In defense of a lot of law enforcement officials who were put in the middle, they were often embarrassed and even apologetic.

When I stood before the magistrate I was not a happy camper and demanded to know what the charges were. The judge could not even look up at me when he told me the charges—"conspiracy to commit loitering." I said to the judge, "I know a lot of Christians who are guilty of that, which basically means 'planning on doing nothing.'" I spent the night in jail, had to pay a bond to get out, and eventually paid a small fine just so I wouldn't have to fly back to Wichita later to fight it in court. I think that defending the charge of "conspiring to loiter" would have been interesting, but it wasn't worth the time.

"They can't do that, can they?" No, but they do it anyway. This was one of the reasons, as pro-life leaders, we had to stay soft in our hearts before the Lord, because it was so easy to get angry and cynical and to lose focus and just get involved in the fight, thus forgetting why we were doing what we were doing. Worship was such a key part of what we did to focus on God and to keep the joy of the Lord in the midst of these heartbreaking situations. Some of the most amazing worship services I've ever experienced were in jail or in front of an "abortuary." My heart goes out to folks who have experienced worship only in a pristine environment.

15

Suffering Loss

We have been very blessed to have had great people in our ministry experiences—sons and daughters in the faith, brothers and sisters who we have been so honored to work with. We have worked with pastors and wives who truly feared God and loved the folks they were serving.

Pastor John Diana had proven to be a capable pastor and a strong teacher, who loved God and loved God's people. He was arrested with me a number of times. Actually, being in jail is a great discipleship opportunity. A great example of that discipleship is Eric Johns, now the renowned pastor of the Buffalo Dream Center. He likes to tell the story of spending a week with me in jail in Florida. The problem was that his wedding was a week away, and he was obviously concerned about getting out in time. He says that I kept telling him not to worry about it—that he could get on the phone and do his vows; he was not comforted! He did get out with two days to spare, however.

One Saturday I told John, "I think they're going to grab me today; they're being aggressive, so be careful. Don't get yourself arrested—someone has to preach tomorrow." The Pittsburgh police at that time were notorious for being out of control to such a degree that a federal judge had to step in and order changes and retraining. I sued them twice for false arrest. I won both times and had the best paydays of my life—$10,000 for a night in jail! So sure enough, they arrested me that day. As they were bringing me into jail, there was John, who had already been arrested. It turns out that the police were beating up on a pro-lifer who was doing nothing and John stepped in and got arrested. He had a sheepish smile on his face. We decided that an empty pulpit may be the best message! The truth is that in the midst of this craziness, our church continued to grow and our leadership was galvanized in unity. There were any number of folks who could preach or teach with a few hours' notice. I preferred John in the pulpit in these situations because I was preparing him to succeed me and wanted to model my trust in him.

As it turned out, we both got out that night. From his drug days, John had hepatitis C and had not taken care of himself. He had also developed a diabetic condition that went undetected and untreated. His life ended way too quickly at the age of 47. We got a call and were shocked that no one knew how serious his condition was—not even him. But in that time he left a great legacy. Penny has always said that he was one of her favorite people. He also taught her how to make his famous spaghetti sauce, which she still makes very regularly and has become "her" famous spaghetti sauce. It seems like spaghetti has had an emotional impact in my life. We still miss John. He was a true spiritual son, and from the day of his salvation until the day of his passing he brought joy to our lives. I know the pain of loss that I have no explanation for—I'm glad I'll see him again.

I had a meeting with Operation Rescue leaders from all over the United States. They flew into Atlanta and, for many of them, it was a real financial sacrifice. They were doing all they could in their communities yet were willing to pitch in to have a national impact. We decided that we would have a national event in Milwaukee. On the way home on the plane, I knew that I had missed the Lord. I believe God had spoken to me about going to Wichita.

I had been doing some study on the abolition movement in Kansas and the Holy Spirit led me to believe that He was going to bless the blood of the martyrs that had been poured out more than a hundred years before to break the back of slavery. Kansas's nickname was "Bleeding Kansas." Farmers and families moved from New York, Ohio, and Pennsylvania to assure that Kansas would not become a slave state. Many were murdered for their efforts to stop slavery.

Now God was speaking to my heart that the seed they had sown was still vibrant and He wanted us to be the water on it. The principle of sowing and reaping is usually considered only on a surface level as it relates to our own lives and circumstances. In Hebrews 7, which specifically refers to tithing, verses 9 and 10 tell us that Levi was blessed by Abraham, even though he was still in Abraham's loins. What one generation does has an effect on another. The teaching in 1 Corinthians 3 tells us that one lays a foundation and another builds on it. A strong look at that text would indicate not just a concurrent blessing but also a generational one can be understood as well. This shows us the power of a generational blessing related to sowing and reaping.

The direction to go to Wichita was one of the strongest words I've ever had; it was extremely clear, and the next thing I had to do took as much courage as anything I've ever done before. I had to organize a conference call with people who had just spent a lot of time and money to come to a meeting where we worked together and decided what we were going to do. I had to tell them that we weren't going to do it any longer. This is not how to effectively lead a team and it certainly impacted people. There were some whom I lost right there and it was hard to be upset or angry with them. There were other godly Christian people who had been there who really did not understand how the Holy Spirit spoke to people in this manner. So it was an uphill battle. Even a couple of my closest confidants advised me not to do this. Although in most cases I would counsel a leader not to move ahead with a change in direction under these circumstances, there are exceptions when you are in a war situation. Decisions have a time stamp. I have often cautioned leaders not to drop the "God told me" bomb. Again, there are times where He really does give divine guidance and if a leader doesn't believe that, he or she probably should not be leading.

Thousands of people ended up coming to Wichita. In one day over eighty pastors were arrested, which was the largest act of non-violent civil disobedience by the clergy in American history. It became a watershed movement. The church was being confronted with the horrors of child sacrifice and God was raising up men and women who understood that it was a gospel issue. The pro-abortion movement took us more seriously than ever. We had planned to be there for a week and now we were there for seven weeks. People just began to come in and help. I still meet people from all over who were awakened because of Wichita.

Mike Haley was one of those guys who came to help. A pastor from Oklahoma, Mike was a hard worker and quickly organized the information of everybody who was in jail and planned how we could communicate with the next of kin. He worked quickly and organized the people around him. It was obvious that there was a leadership mantle upon his life. During the next couple of weeks we got to know each other, and that's when I found out about Mike's ministry as a pastor and a teacher. In one of our next outreaches in Baton Rouge, Louisiana (we had thousands of people there), I had Mike serve as one of the main speakers. The copies of his teaching were the most requested we've ever had. Mike was in the process of turning his church in Ardmore, Oklahoma, over to one of his sons in the faith. He invited me to come down and speak, and that's when I got to know his family and some of the people in his church. As I said, we've been blessed to be around a lot of top-quality people. Mike Haley was at the top of that list; we were making plans to work together. He was a gifted communicator with a wonderful sense of humor. He was one of those guys who could do anything.

I had recently relocated back to Pennsylvania and asked Mike to join me there. We were very excited about this. He brought his whole family and stayed with us for a week. Out of the blue, Mike was diagnosed with aggressive cancer—and lost his battle at the age of 47 (the same age at which John, mentioned a few paragraphs previously, died). My heart was so grieved. I saw Mike as a ministry partner you could only dream about. Mature, seasoned, a successful pastor—make a list and you could check the box. When you have to lead the funeral of someone whose death is simply beyond any human explanation, you need the comforter, the Holy Spirit Himself. When the pallbearers spontaneously lifted his casket above their heads while carrying him out as the congregation sang "Shout to Lord," it was an experience those who were there never forgot. The loss was very real.

At one time we moved our whole family to Melbourne, Florida, to do a special pro-life training called "Impact Team," consisting of twenty-three students from around the country who came for a three-month training exercise. We spent time in prayer and had incredible guest teachers to educate us—doctors, lawyers, theologians, and historians. It was an amazing time. We spread out to small communities in Florida that had killing centers and mobilized believers. During that time six abortion businesses were shut down because of our presence.

Most of these places are like rodents—they do all they can to avoid detection. Our strategy was to call attention to them. Of course, they never put an "Abortions Performed Here" sign out front. Instead, they use something like "Main Street Gynecology." In one case we dealt with an abortion center in a strip mall. We went to all the neighboring businesses, and apparently none of them were aware of what was going on until we showed up. The place next door to the abortion center was none other than a day care center! We were able to get a list of all the daycare families and sent them letters showing how they were advertising abortion in neighboring communities, which was not an uncommon practice. In all my years I'm not aware of one abortionist who lived in the community where they killed children. Once word got out, the landlord cancelled the lease of the abortion center in order to keep the rest of his tenants. I don't know how many of the other businesses had pro-life owners, but we learned quickly that very, very few wanted to be associated in any way with a killing center.

One of my practices during our pro-life campaigns was to always take time to meet with pastors to let them know that I fully supported them and to be available to them in any way I could. My objective was to give them the benefit of firsthand information so that they wouldn't get it from the media.

In one of those meetings there was a guy in the very back row with his chair leaning back, hands folded, just taking the meeting in. The Holy Spirit clearly said to me, "I sent you here for him." Please understand that I didn't have these kinds of words every day of my life or every week, every month, maybe not every year. I'm sharing with you the highlights of very significant things that happened in forty-plus years of ministry and the fact that God did indeed speak and still does speak to his people—He intervenes! I'm not trying to over-dramatize it in any way, nor do I want you to believe that these dramatic things happened on a regular basis, but when they did, it proved to be very significant.

His name was Luther and he turned out to be one of the finest men I've ever met in my life. He was a guy you would want to go into the foxhole with you. Under his casual facade was a church scholar with a prophetic voice. He pastored a small church while he and his wife raised seven children and ran a business.

Our entire families became intermingled. Penny and Patti (Luther's wife), became wonderful friends and great supports for each another. We jumped into church life together and three years later, when I left, the church had grown significantly during my time there. He had yielded the lead pastor role to me, but now I turned it back to him. He was a clear thinker with very deep convictions and great insight into situations. Luther had served in the Navy and had asbestos poisoning in his lungs, which caused him to be short of breath and to have to limit his physical exertion at times. On most days when you were around him, though, you would never know there was anything wrong.

After we moved back to Pennsylvania, the asbestos poisoning became more chronic, and unbelievably Luther lost his life at age 48. It was so painful for Penny and me. The pain of losing three incredible men (John, Mike, and Luther) who had become so close to us, so important to us, and so completely valuable to the kingdom was beyond comprehension. I cried out to the Lord and asked, "How do you replace people like this? They were rare by any way you assess them—and now they're gone and I'm still here!"

To this day I don't know how I made it through. I guess I thought about their families, who had suffered far worse than we had. It was hard to feel sorry for myself based on that. I often wonder today what life would have been like if I still had those men in my life. To have had all of them together at one time would have been unbelievable—what a team that would have been!

The lessons learned are that life is valuable, life is fragile, and life is precious. There are days that I long for heaven and I question why I'm here and these men are gone, but at the end of the day it just increases my conviction about how valuable and precious each individual life is. I can remember meeting guys who were near the age of 47 or 48 and telling them, "Hey—you really don't want to be around me. I've lost too many friends your age."

Jesus said that the wheat and tares grow together. I understand that I've seen God's power in amazing ways that are undeniable. I've sat in the dark, broken beyond description. I know what it's like to abound and what it's like to be abased. I am a follower, and He is Lord. He does not change.

CHAPTER

——— **16** ———

Another Assignment

Jay Sekulow called me and told me that I needed to come to D.C. The Senate was trying to pass a law—a piece of legislation called FACE (*Freedom to Access Clinic Entrances*). This would make blocking an abortion clinic a civil rights violation with both a civil and criminal penalty. Jay wanted to prepare me for testimony. I was being subpoenaed by the Senate judiciary committee. The short story is that the FACE legislation passed and became the firewall against Operation Rescue. It did what they had tried to get RICO to do. Now, just for being outside a clinic, even if you didn't break a law, if you "impeded or restricted the egress or the progress of somebody seeking an abortion," you could be guilty of a federal violation with civil and criminal charges.

When I testified in front of the Senate, one member of the Senate and I got into quite a lively debate. At that point I had been going full throttle for four years, had undergone numerous arrests, and been the object of over ten lawsuits. I had been beat up, had guns pulled on me, and certainly had the press absolutely lie about me and other nonviolent pro-lifers. I had watched great people suffer much and had spent way too much time away from home and my family. I had surrendered a thriving church in obedience to God's call but had also experienced God's heart and met some of the most precious, godly people ever.

Months later I was on a red-eye flight back home. The flight was not full and I was able to spread out across the seats. By the time I got home, I knew the grace to lead in my present capacity had come to an end. Just prior to that, several abortion doctors had been gunned down—certainly not by anyone working with us. But there were folks in our ranks who were now talking about justifiable homicide. When I testified at the FACE hearings, one of my comments was that if you do not stand and protect free speech and you criminalize non-criminal behavior because you do not like the content of the speech, then you are opening the door for people to use violence.

That's exactly what was happening. I took a very strong stand for nonviolence. We had always made people sign a nonviolent declaration if they were going to participate—that was always part of what we did. Now I pulled the leaders together and told them that I wanted to renew that statement and make it even stronger. I got pushback.

I realized that although I was right in my head and my theology was correct, my heart was becoming full of anger. The depth of the entrenchment of the abortion culture in the courts, police departments, legislature, and media shocked us. Very few of those people ever celebrated us or gave us any credit. More hurtful were the many churches who would not help but rather spoke against us. That was always like a knife to my heart, because I know how much God loves His church. To see it turn its back on the least of these would be far worse than anything else I had experienced up to this point. I knew I could not continue leading with such anger in my heart. I now understood why generals were rotated from the battlefront. I still had vision and commitment. The greatest motivation I had in pro-life leadership was to see the Lord pleased with His church.

I continued preaching as invitations came in, and those kept me engaged. Penny and I were regrouping; we had moved back from Florida right around the time that my mom died and worked on the old farmhouse we had purchased. It was pretty rough—that first winter everything in our cupboards froze. We had record-setting snowfall, and our van could not make it up and down the driveway without some extra help. I wrapped a chain through the frame and hung it on the bumper; then Penny would get into the van and I drove an old pick-up truck to tow her up the driveway. Actually, things were going pretty well for us. I had a lot of invitations to speak and was able to support my family. It was the first time in ministry that I did not have to run an organization.

The churches I had previously pastored and others we had helped to start also continued being generous to us. Of course, I was still speaking about God's heart for the unborn and was doing leadership seminars as well as helping church planters. I was enjoying a season of refreshment. A local group who were leaving the United Methodist church because of their funding of abortion asked if I could help with a church plant. This was close to where I lived and the small group seemed to be properly focused. I told them I would consider it on two conditions: number one, we actually would plant a church in a nearby town, where there would be more opportunity; and number two, we would pursue the New Testament model found in Ephesians 2 of building our lives together for God's habitation. I told them that I would commit to helping them for six months to put things together and that with my contacts I would find a young man whom I would mentor to become the pastor. Everybody was excited about the plan.

One time I was in California preaching and Gary, a well-known prophetic guy from the area, came to the Sunday night service. He said, "I'm so glad to see you; I have a word for you." He gave me Proverbs 12:11 (NASB): "He who works his land will have plenty of bread, but one who pursues worthless things lacks sense." Instantly I knew what it meant—that Penny and I were supposed to commit ourselves to that fledging church. This was during the most peaceful time I had had in ministry in years, and we were doing quite well financially due to the fact that the people in the places we were going were being very generous to us.

I must admit that the thought of starting all over again financially was not appealing. I would have to stop traveling, and church plants don't have resources needed to take care of a family. We were up to eight kids now. I guess that's why God used Gary to speak to me. Maybe it was something I really wasn't excited about. I called home and told Penny, "I got a word," and I told her what had been shared with me. She knew who he was and, before I could tell her anything, she told me that she knew we were supposed to commit ourselves to this church plant. She was actually very excited about it. So that closed the door on my backing out.

For the next fifteen years that's what we did. Once again the Lord treated us wonderfully. I never did make the money I had given up, but neither did we suffer. We saw God's hand move in many ways, and most important of all, we were surrounded by a church body who loved us, loved each other, loved God, and loved the world. Penny was deeply involved in helping to pastor the church and was more than effective, in her element—loving and training people in the church with great passion.

About a year and a half before we stepped down, I was speaking at a conference where one of the ministers there, Doug Allen, had spent five years in Russia doing church planting—something near and dear to my heart. He and his wife, Paula, were seeking God as to their next step. I knew them a little from having spoken at their home church years before. The Lord put it on my heart to invite them to Living Hope to speak for the purpose of blessing them. I told our leaders about my invitation.

I usually didn't leave when we had guest ministry in, but something had come up. My only instructions were to give him a big offering. What a joy to work with generous people! They loved Doug's ministry and we got great reports. As we sought God about our replacement, we had a couple of things we had considered that were not working out. This was new to me, as

I had always known who should succeed me in other situations.

The Alliance Defending Freedom had called and said they were doing a lawyers' cruise and had a couple spots open. Penny and I could have one for free if we wanted it. We have never been on a cruise and this sounded very exciting to me. I also was looking for some time alone with the Lord to study and to really seek the direction for Living Hope Church. I also heard that you really eat well on a cruise! I met with our church leaders before I left and said, "Please be praying that when we get back I'll have the word of the Lord and know what to do regarding our direction for the next pastor."

Though they were not anxious to get rid of me, we were prepared and they wanted to do all they could to help us move on to our next assignment. I also had put some things on hold so that the new pastor would not have to inherit a lot of projects he was not excited about. The church leaders were enthusiastic about my coming back with clear direction. The only problem was that when we got home from the cruise, I did not have the direction from the Holy Spirit that I had earnestly expected. I was more bewildered than upset.

A couple of nights after our return home, we drove up to visit our son and his wife. On the way back, while Penny and I were talking, in the middle of our conversation the word of the Lord came to me and told me there was something I had to do regarding a situation in our church. I committed to doing that, and in the morning I handled it.

Almost immediately the Lord brought Doug and Paula Allen to my heart. They were driving to a mission's conference and were going to meet with somebody about re-launching back into Russia. I called Doug and he told me that when he saw my name pop up on his phone, he knew what I was going to ask him to pray about coming to serve at Living Hope Church.

We met with the team and told them what I had thrown out; they were excited. In a matter of weeks Doug and Paula had packed up their stuff and were coming to Living Hope Church. They are another example of the type of people who we are incredibly blessed just to know and love. They have loved the church and Doug probably has one of the best senses of humor of any human being I've ever met. They've been generous and kind to Penny and me. This Ephesians 2 stuff works!

My new assignment was with the Network of Related Pastors, a group of men who had come to work together over the years. I had known many of them through pro-life and mission activities, and I was asked to step in as a second in command. Pastoring pastors is a real privilege; after five years I assumed the lead role. We continue to address the pro-life battle and are actively engaging the culture on many fronts.

CHAPTER

—17—

We Have a Living Hope

Now that we had received the call to work with this small group who was leaving the United Methodist church, it was time to go to work. I had to call places where I had scheduled to speak and ask them to release me from those engagements. I had never really done that before and can only remember several times when I cancelled a commitment. There were times I wanted to cancel because I just wanted to stay home, or other more prestigious or inviting opportunities would present themselves. I was tempted, but I tried to maintain a kingdom attitude and honor the assignment I was given, trusting God that He would take care of the rest.

One thing I've struggled with is in regard to periods when I've sacrificed time with my family, prepared myself for a ministry time (preaching and teaching, meeting with leaders, developing mission strategies), later realizing that the truths and things that I had labored to impart were not followed through on. If you dwell on it, it can be pretty discouraging to see folks drop the ball after you've been invited somewhere and given your all to help in specific areas of need. I have had more than one late Sunday night flight home, asking God if we accomplished anything besides getting people excited for a few hours. Please hear me—I know inspiration is valid, needed, and important. But when you toil to develop a plan to help leaders move forward and it's neglected and forgotten, it can wear on you. Of course, that struggle is not much different than the men and women who faithfully go to work each week hoping not just to earn the funds to take care of their family but also to make a difference in what they do.

It's important for spiritual leaders to remind themselves about the folks in the trenches who cause churches and ministries to run. These folks are also contributing so much of their lives in the hopes that God will be glorified and people's lives changed. It concerns me that there is a prima donna attitude that sometimes invades ministry—forgetting that we are soldiers, not professors.

Early in my ministry during one of the first pastor's conferences I spoke at (even before Operation Rescue), I was confused by the fact that one of the other speakers who, of course, was much more accomplished and known than I was, had told the conference host that he had to have a hotel room just for the couple of hours that he would be there so he could have private restroom facilities and would not have to mingle with folks—just speak and leave. He also had some other requests: fresh fruit in the room and so on. Listen: I think we should honor men and women who speak God's Word into our lives—being generous, kind, and thoughtful. I like it when I get a call or an email from a church ahead of time asking me what kind of food I like and what snacks they can put in my room—that's thoughtful. But it's different than requesting it yourself or even demanding it.

I've been to places where the hospitality has been lacking, but we must focus on the honor of speaking God's Word and remind ourselves that it's a privilege to be there. All of us are flattered when folks fuss over us to show their appreciation, but let's not forget that we are soldiers and there are people we are speaking to who have been overlooked and who very seldom have someone go out of their way to pamper them. My dear friend and spiritual son Pastor Rick Paladin frequently has a stash of gift cards he puts into people's hands to remind them of how valued they are. I like that!

Often after being at a church I'll bless someone in that congregation who I'm aware is really giving all or going through a hard time. There have been times I've just signed the back of the honorarium check and then given it to the person and told him or her that it's just between us. I try to do things on purpose that will keep me from being self-centered.

Now Penny and I were starting a church and giving up our time, schedules, and income. We had done this before but that was years earlier. Now we had a house full of kids. David and Anne Drye, wonderful, godly folks whom God had blessed through their hard work, took us on as missionaries. Ed and Mary, a business couple who were members of Word and Worship, did the same. We didn't know that was going to happen—Penny and I were simply moving in faith.

Remember the losses I told you about earlier? One day when I was sitting at my dining room table opening the mail, there in my hand was a check from David and Anne. Then the phone rang. Jeff, a friend from California, told me that the Dryes had just died together in a plane crash. I had the check in one hand and the phone in another. Another question for heaven.

To illustrate how generous these people were, David went to the Soviet Union with me. He wanted to witness the revival that was breaking out. There in the Soviet Union I spoke at a pastors' and mission leaders' conference. This was a new day in the Soviet Union, so these types of event were remarkable to them. About thirty folks were in attendance. David gave each of them $5,000. I had no idea that he was going to do that. Can you imagine how that impacted them? After their deaths, David's son-in-law asked me what commitment David and Anne had made to Penny and me. I told them, and they honored that through David's business, so we had eighteen months of a support base—certainly not all we needed, but a big boost! Thank you, Dave and Anne. Once again, God had intervened in our lives as we attempted to follow Him.

We named the church "Living Hope Church" and our little group began growing. Among them were Ralph and Pat, who were older and mature believers. I had met them years before when I was pastoring Word and Worship, which was about thirty miles away. They had come to see me about opening a crisis pregnancy center. I don't even remember the meeting, but apparently we were able to help them. So here we were, full circle. They each had a pastor's heart and were full of the Word. Every church plant should have a Ralph and a Pat! We worked great as a team. Ralph worked for the electric company and was close to retirement. Pat was full-time at the crisis pregnancy center and part of Penny's leadership team. They had a heart for missions and were so excited to be on the ground floor of a church with a missions DNA. Ralph retired and gave a lot of his time to the church. They were exploring different missions opportunities and desired to go to the mission field together, but it never happened. Ralph lost his battle for life but finished well. Pat amazingly fulfilled their dream by going to Indonesia herself for almost a year.

In just a couple of years we were able to purchase property and build a nice worship facility. We were there for fifteen years and have great friends and co-laborers we worked together with. Pastor Doug and Paula Allen took over for us. They had served five years in Russia as church planters and pastors. I had met them years before while speaking at the church they were on staff at—a perfect fit. I still speak at the church several times a year and Penny and I enjoy great friendship and fellowship with the saints there.

CHAPTER

—— **18** ——

Lessons to Learn

When you read a book about someone's life, he or she, of course, is going to give you the highlights. That's what I'm doing—giving you the overview or the good stories. I've been disappointed many times and have learned that the saddest people are those who are never disappointed because they never expect much. I've also learned that there's a big difference between disappointment and discouragement. We must refuse discouragement—it leaves us without courage. My greatest desire is that you can believe God for intervention in your life. Trust me: I've had some low spots, made some bad decisions, exhibited some bad attitudes, and also committed some bad actions—sin! Acknowledging God's grace is more than admitting weakness or even confessing sin. Grace is not divine slack—it's divine power to overcome. Grace always calls us to grow.

Our obligation as believers is not to be flawless but rather to respond to our flaws in light of true empowering grace. When we see ourselves and our behavior or attitudes short of scriptural standards or when the Holy Spirit calls us to account, we must, as followers of Jesus, pursue Him for victory. So I want to share some important lessons I've learned.

Lesson 1: Anger is an emotion that is not entirely unholy.
God is angry at particular things. Jesus was angry at times. In fact, the church as a whole has lost the heart to be angry at what God is angry about. Proverbs 6:16–19 (NASB) points out,

> There are six things that the Lord hates, Seven that are an abomination to Him: Haughty eyes, a lying tongue, And hands that shed innocent blood, A heart that devises wicked plans, Feet that run rapidly to evil, A false witness who declares lies, And one who spreads strife among brothers.

It seems the church gets stirred up with things that are on God's heart—things that are important to him—but then we can easily get distracted. I think we've earned a reputation in the world and political structures that, while we may make a little noise, soon we go back to our church meetings. Personal anger is a whole other story. When anger is only emotional and not about righteousness, it will bubble over into sin. Here's what I know about emotional anger—it's just plain selfish, whether it's toward your wife, your kids, or your boss. Ultimately it's about you not getting your own way!

I spent years trying to manage my anger, often justifying it because of someone else's failures or actions. Even after I would repent over an outburst, like chronic sin, it would visit again. After a particularly devastating outburst that hurt a lot of people (none more than my family), I finally came to a place of real understanding. I was reading a Watchman Nee book, *Changed into His Likeness*, and it just hit me how selfish anger is. I never liked selfish people. At that point, I didn't like me. Anger is just self-will pouting over not getting its own way—ugh! This is not to say I haven't been angry since, but the playing field has changed. I see the enemy more clearly, and from a greater distance! It used to frustrate me, even surprise me, how I could get ambushed. I'm now usually aware of when I'm being tempted to make it all about me.

Lesson 2: Slow down! Pace yourself. I was never good about taking breaks; there was always so much to do. I was never really driven by what others thought I should do, but rather, my own expectations were more than enough to keep me going a hundred miles an hour. I detest laziness and see it as a sin that has become acceptable. In Ephesians 4 Paul writes about the "work" of the ministry. I always tell people that the Greek word for the word *work* is *work*. There will always be more work than time or energy.

Here's the thing: I would rather work than do nothing. I've heard all the sermons and heard so many older ministers say what I needed to hear and to do about taking time off and getting refreshed. I would agree—but then not do it. There are certain seasons in your life when you need to savor and just slow down. Keep going forward, but slow down. The Sabbath principle is designed to keep us fresh, not just restore us when we are exhausted. When the pro-life movement intensified in Wichita, I was consumed for five weeks (eighteen-hour days more often than not). The federal judge had me arrested for disobeying his order; they put me in a single cell in the jail. I woke up a day and half later! The guards told me they had checked on me several times out of concern that I was having a health issue. I've never been a sound sleeper or a long one, but that's how hard you can push yourself. There are some seasons in life that demand you take a break. I was always a pretty decent planner but never planned breaks. Taking a break is like saving for the future.

Lesson 3: Become a listener. Most strong leaders are fixers. Unfortunately, while another person is talking, they're already thinking of a solution. They hear words but they miss the emotion, the context, the dimension, the nuance. I can't tell you how many times Penny would speak to me after a meeting and tell me something she heard that I didn't hear at all. That's not a good quality. Ask yourself, "What did I hear? What is this person trying to say?"—rather than "What do I need to do?" As I have employed this, I think I've become a much better leader. I think I've earned people's trust because they see my heart and realize that I really do care. One of the universal languages is listening. Ask those around you if you are perceived to be a good listener—then brace yourself for the answer!

Lesson 4: Be a giver. One of the greatest points of agreement in our marriage is that we've decided to always be givers. Whatever blessings in our life that God has given us, whether it's our home, our time, or money, we want to be givers. I don't trust stingy leaders or stingy Christians. People who don't tithe steal from God, according to Malachi 3:8. Anyone who steals from God is capable of stealing from you! What we do with our money really is a reflection of what's in our hearts. Jesus said, "Where your treasure is, there your heart will be also." Giving of the three T's—our time, our talent, and our treasure—should be treated as an opportunity, not an irritation. You don't have to say yes all the time, but your mindset should be a green light. Then if the Lord flashes you the yellow light or a red light, you simply put on the brakes. I believe we can give our way into a better place, just as I believe we can pray or serve our way into a better place.

Several years ago on a Saturday night I got a call about a missionary friend who had been devastated by a hurricane. I started calling pastors asking if they would receive a special offering the next morning. It's very hard to get pastors on the phone on a Saturday, but I worked hard, and by the end of the evening, twenty churches had agreed to receive an offering, and thousands of dollars came in during the next two weeks. I was away preaching that weekend. As I lay back on my bed at the hotel, feeling pretty proud of myself, it was as if the Holy Spirit tapped me and said, "What are you going to do?" My thought was "Lord, I just raised all that money." When you are challenged to be more generous than what seems normal, I doubt that it's the devil. Before I knew it, I was calling Penny and telling her I wanted to give my skid loader tractor away. I had saved for a long time to buy that tractor. We lived out in the country and I used it to keep our driveway maintained and to move snow in the winter. In my opinion it was the ultimate man toy. She said, "Sure, that's good with me—are you going to buy another one?" The answer was "No." She said, "Fine—go for it." I called our mission director at home and told him to get it out of there; I never wanted to see it again. I was afraid I would change my mind. My sons all vividly remember it. Today they're big givers, and they bring the tractor story up from time to time. Learn to give your way out of yourself. Pastor Joe Warner, who was organizing some relief efforts, had it put onto a barge with hurricane relief supplies.

Lesson 5: Always be submitted. You should always be submitted, and I don't mean in name only. Is there anyone who can speak into your life—for real? Some of my greatest failures happened when people who should have spoken into my life didn't, or when I was unwilling to listen to people who hinted around. Likewise, be a friend who speaks the truth in love. If you're accountable, then the people around you should know what that looks like and whom you're accountable to. It should be someone who cares about you and you can think out loud with. If you have a strong personality, like me, you'll need a strong, clear voice. One of the evidences of a conscientious leader is the desire for accountability structure and relationships with other leaders. One of the things I love about the Network of Related Pastors is this kind of relationship.

Lesson 6: Cherish people. I grew up moving through life without any lifelong friends and a distant family. It's easy to do the same in life and ministry. There are people who don't have to be part of your organization or help you do what you do—they're just your friends. Cherish them. Honor that inner circle. If you're blessed, you have a really good friend or even two. But don't neglect the others who are passing through your life—keep in touch.

Lesson 7: Follow and feed your convictions. Feed the things that you feel strongly about. Feed your intellect—develop your thinking, study to show yourself approved, even if it's just for your own enjoyment. It will make you a more fruitful person. Act out your convictions and put your life out there. Stand up and refuse to be intimidated.

CHAPTER
——————19——————

Old Friends—New Challenges

I picked up the phone. "Brother Keith?" I knew that deep voice filled with Cajun spice. It was Brother Rod, as he is affectionately known. "I need to talk with you." Pastor Rod Aguillard pastored a thriving church outside New Orleans. We met in jail years earlier during the Democratic National Convention in Atlanta after being arrested for sitting down in front of death centers. Several hundred of us had been thrown into a gym that was converted into a makeshift jail. We preached, prayed, and worshiped. It was obvious that Brother Rod was a guy who meant business, which was evident by a group of pastors he had led there who looked to him as a spiritual father. He and I became great friends. We talked from time to time and saw each other at pro-life gatherings, and he occasionally invited me down to the church he pastored. This phone call was seventeen years after our initial jail meeting.

A group of pastors were starting an organization of non-denominational churches where there could be a mechanism for working together, having a united voice and ministerial accountability. They wanted me to be a part of it. Brother Rod came up to talk to Penny and me about it, and we agreed that it was a great privilege to work with a man I highly respected and with other true pastors. I didn't know that almost fifteen years later Brother Rod and the team would hand the leadership over to me. The relationships that have been formed, the missions accomplished, and lives that have been transformed have made this a wonderful journey.

Working with pastors in some ways is like working with any other group of people. You must love them and want the best for them. You must comprehend, despite great gifting and leadership, that they are mere humans like the rest of us. As the saying goes, "They put their pants on just like everyone else: one leg at a time." They're like other Christians—they want to be a part of what God is doing, with folks who love and trust each another and walk through life together. I think that if most church members could understand this, our churches would be healthier.

What's different about pastors as a group is that they are all leaders! I've told people that it's like coaching a team full of quarterbacks. Sometimes I feel as if I'm directing traffic at an eight-way intersection. I would not have it any other way. That's what leaders do—they lead. Penny and I count it an honor to be trusted, to hear their hearts, and to be involved in their lives often far beyond church business and activities. The culture that the Network of Related Pastors has developed is life-giving, rich, and nourishing. In the last few years we have developed several conferences, which we do each year, and we can't wait until we get there to see each other. Thanks to the generosity of these leaders, their churches, and others, we have a staff who absolutely loves what they are doing in serving the local churches. One of the highlights of my travels is getting special time with younger couples who are serving and preparing for ministry. Our country needs a lot of help, but nothing more than a new generation of uncompromising leaders.

CHAPTER

—— **20** ——

I'm Never Broke—
I Always Have a Penny

'm never broke—I always have a Penny! Penny and I have been married for forty-two years. We have eight children—five girls and three boys. We love them to pieces. We also currently have fourteen grandkids with hopefully more on the way.

Penny's dad left her mom and moved in with a lady up the street when Penny was 13 years old. Her two older sisters were out of the house and she and her younger brother were left to her mom's care. Her mom, Elaine, was a wonderful and godly lady. At 92 she came to live with us and was with us almost two years before she went to be with Jesus. She never remarried. She worked as a custodian at a bank, cleaned folks' houses, and worked at a health food store, though she didn't exactly adhere to that lifestyle—she loved Hershey bars and raisin-filled cookies!

Penny went through the typical teen rebellion stuff, but she was a good student and was greatly influenced by her mom. Elaine's church brought in the Teen Challenge choir every year. Although they had little to spare, Elaine would always offer to take a few of the boys from the choir for the night, feed them, and get them to the church services.

The boys who came, of course, paid attention to Penny—what young guy wouldn't? They discussed with her the importance of a relationship with Jesus and talked her into coming to church. That Sunday night at church she made a public confession of faith in Christ and has never looked back.

Shortly after that time, I came into the church—what great timing!—and we became friends. Her mom invited a few of us young guys without families over for dinner sometimes on Sunday afternoons. I would never have imagined that one day Penny would be my wife. I had become extremely attracted to her and very interested in dating her. I saw things in her that were unique and very appealing. One day when I was visiting her I came right out with the sentiment: "I'm here to let you know that I like you!" Being very straightforward, I immediately asked for a response. She gave me a try and two years later we were married in our home church in Trafford, Pennsylvania.

There have certainly been times of struggles. When we married I was 22 and she was 21, and I was still more rough around the edges than I understood. The unhealed struggles in my life were still impacting me in many ways. I was not always understanding or affirming, and the truth is, I was often harsh. The Holy Spirit can work only on what we acknowledge. I struggled to see my flaws. As I look back now, I can see them, but then—not so much.

Despite this, we kept loving and learning. It seems we always did well on the big stuff but often let the little things upset us. Life is fragile; each of us needs more tender loving care than we realize and often the people in our lives need us to care for them more than we realize.

I've loved her with all my heart all these years. I wish my skills of loving well had matured quicker. Wherever I go to speak I'm asked if Penny is coming. "Where's Penny?" is the constant question. I call them the "Penny

Fan Club." Sometimes I tell her that I should stay home and send her out to speak.

Although she doesn't really love being in front of a crowd to speak, she is a very good communicator and has impacted many people through what she has said to them. She is passionate about and teaches about our heritage as a nation and the responsibility we have as believers to see that legacy continue. She once did a history series for the youth in the church when she realized how bankrupt their public school education had left them in regard to their nation's Christian heritage. They loved it and could not get enough of it. She planned a guided tour for her and our kids to Washington, D.C., by a well-versed historian, who pointed out many of the biblical inscriptions throughout the nation's capital. That is one of her passions. Colonial Williamsburg is one of her favorite places to go. Once during a conversation with a pastor and his wife, the subject of who had a greater world impact, Ronald Reagan or Winston Churchill, came up. I said Churchill; she got annoyed with me, insisting that Reagan was on par with Churchill. When she goes out and talks to groups, invariably it will come down to the love of God and loving others. She has a great revelation of our Father's heart, which empowers us to love one another, and her audiences love to hear her share it.

Penny loves small-group settings and being connected—not just for fellowship but action as well. When I served as a pastor I would often turn to her for help with projects and areas of ministry that needed attention. Her team would spring into action and make things happen. One of her favorite activities is building a strong, well-equipped team and helping others with the desire to do so. She's written on it and coached others many times. Unlike me, Penny has an artistic gift. She's good musically and can paint and draw. She writes poems. Fortunately, our kids have inherited her side more than mine. I'm amazed by that type of gift; I have none of it.

Penny is steady and faithful, like a built-in equilibrium. Through all the outward things we've been through, all the unknowns, all the attacks and challenges, she has been the picture of consistency. I always tell people that you are blessed if God sends a prophet into your life. If you're *really* blessed, you get to *marry* the prophet! She has been a voice of wisdom, a voice of caution, a voice of courage. She is the "take the shirt off your back" person we all want to be. To know her is to love her! There have been many days that people weren't always so sure about *me*, but she was my equity; she still is. *I'm never broke—I have a Penny!*

Go Long

Every kid who plays football wants to be the quarterback. Working with leaders is like having a room full of quarterbacks. Of course, working with a leader who doesn't think he or she should be the quarterback presents a different set of challenges. But when that person gets the ball, more often than not he or she is thinking—"Go long"! Never mind the fact that the player can't heave the ball to where the receiver can get to it.

Life is a "go long" proposition. We all love the big-game comebacks. I'm a baseball fan. The 1960 Pittsburgh Pirates beat the mighty New York Yankees in the world series. Bill Mazeroski, who was known for his fielding, hit a ninth-inning home run for late-inning heroics. The Yankees had won three games by a score of 16 to 3, 10 to 0, and 12 to 0. But somehow the Pirates managed to win the other four games by close scores. The picture of Bill Mazeroski coming around third base while waving his hat is iconic.

The Pittsburgh Steelers were a hapless football organization—the lovable losers. But then in 1976 a remarkable thing happened. They actually made it to the playoffs. There one of those famous plays in football history happened with no time left on the clock. Terry Bradshaw threw the ball down the field to go long. The ball ricocheted off several players and was scooped by Franco Harris. Running down the sidelines just before it hit the ground with no time on the clock, the Steelers won their first playoff game in forty years. That led to four Super Bowls in a six-year span. When you go through the Pittsburgh airport, as I do almost every week, you see two statues at the top of the escalator—one of George Washington (whose hub of historic activity was the Pittsburgh area) and the other of Franco Harris scooping the ball before it hit the ground! *Go long go for the win!*

We're sad when we see a person, a family, a church, or a business have a great run only to fade and fail in the end. Christians who fall away from their faith are the greatest tragedy. Sometimes we think this is just a current phenomenon. However, the Scriptures are full of warnings not to fade and examples of folks who did. I've seen people quit when the finish line was close, after they had already endured and invested much. Ephesians 4:23 tells us not to give up but to be renewed in the spirit of our minds. The command not to faint, or give up, tells me that the temptation to give up and quit is a spiritual struggle. "Don't do it!" is an appeal not to the flesh but to the spirit to see the finish line. Although we have much kingdom work to do on this planet and the cares of life to negotiate, we must "go long." We must think about crossing the finish line leaving this place, having been faithful.

At one point while we were living in Florida, I received a phone call from my sister, Debbie, about our mom, who was dying. She had battled lung cancer for several years without major complications, but it seemed that it was now catching up with her, and she was only 68. I was going to be in New York in a few days, so going to Pittsburgh would be no problem. She was in a hospital when I went to see her, sitting in bed with her face made up and hair fixed. This didn't surprise me; she was always concerned about how she looked. She was always a petite person, but now she was frail. We had a nice time together and I came back the next day. My plane would leave later that afternoon. I guess we both knew this was probably going to be the last time we would see each other here on earth. I was choked up but held it together.

Our relationship really had been redeemed and I was confident that she was ready for heaven. God had intervened.

Finally it was time to go. I prayed with her, hugged her, and said goodbye. I walked down the hall to the elevator more numb than anything, got onto the elevator, and as I pushed the button to go down, it was as if the Holy Spirit tapped me on the shoulder and made me ponder, What are you doing? I hit the "open" button and escaped before the elevator could move. The doors popped open and I ran down the hall into her room and just buried my face in her bony shoulder. By this time I was not holding it together. I was in a full sob—my face and shirt soaked with tears. She just patted my back.

Finally, when I was able to get somewhat composed, I was able to speak. It was now really clear that this was our last moment together on earth. Then she said something startling to me: "You have been such a delight!" All those years of anger, estrangement, and pain seemed to just vanish. To this day when I talk of those childhood pains related to her, they are just facts, as if I'm talking about somebody else. O death, where is your sting? As I turned to leave again, she smiled big and said, "Tell Penny I said congratulations." We had recently found out that we were expecting our seventh child, whom we would name Jessie. I love the fact that those were my mom's last words, and I've mentioned it to Jessie more than once. As I made my way to the elevator and regained my emotional equilibrium, the only thought that kept coming to me was how wonderful it felt to hear those words from my mom. Then I thought about how it will feel to hear someday, "Well done, good and faithful servant!" from Jesus.

Go long! Finish faithful! Don't quit! Don't give in or give up! I can't help but believe that if folks could understand the reality of that, they would have the strength to finish—not by will power but by a heavenly push into the arms of Jesus!

Where are you right now? It's important, but it's not as important as where God has called you to go and what He has promised to say to you one day. I believe that if we could hear those words, we could run to the finish. If we could remember those who finished well—some alone and unappreciated, people whom the world was not worthy of—we would not only finish but also flourish. He is the God who intervened for me and saved me from sin, saved me from myself, and saved me for Himself. My greatest motivation in preaching the gospel is that I know that what He did for me He will do for you.

Do not allow your life to be measured by this vapor we call life. Eternity is real. We will stand before no committee, no witness, no one to plead our case, and when we look at Him, every sin resisted, every command obeyed, every leading followed, every prayer said and dime given, every act of kindness and forgiveness will seem magnified in the light of being with Him forever. Go long, my friend—go long.

About the Author

Keith Tucci is the Apostolic Team Leader for the Network of Related Pastors, a pastor, church planter, missionary, and voice for the unborn. His passion for the local church and his care and concern for its leaders have endeared him to many pastors and their families around the globe. He is frequently called upon for strategic assistance and leadership development, and he has been involved in church planting efforts both in the United States and abroad.

Keith has done extensive missions work in Eastern Europe and was arrested twice in the former Soviet Union for ministering to persecuted leaders. He sits on several missions boards and consults with mission organizations and local churches to raise up mission movements.

For four years, Keith served as the director of Operation Rescue, a national anti-abortion organization. He was a part of numerous abortion clinic blockades, resulting in many arrests for challenging judicial tyranny and free speech violations.

Keith has appeared as a guest on a number of media outlets to articulate a Christian worldview in response to a number of cultural issues. These appearances have included all the national network news shows including *Nightline, Good Morning America,* and, most notably, *Firing Line* with Dr. William Buckley.

Keith has been both the main plaintiff and defendant in a number of national cases because of his outspoken advocacy for the unborn and the Christian family. Two of these cases have resulted in victories at the Supreme Court level, as well as several other victorious actions against those who would try to impede the preaching of the gospel beyond the walls of the Church.

Keith and his wife, Penny, have been married for 43 years. They have 8 children and 14 grandchildren. Penny is an integral part of their ministry together. She has trained and mentored strong women's leadership teams within local churches.